JU ‑23

Sixty-first year of publication

Contributors:
Rodney Pettinga
Richard Young

RACING POST

Commissioned by RACING POST, Floor 7, Vivo Building South Bank Central,
30 Stamford Street, London, SE1 9LS

First published in 2022 by PITCH PUBLISHING Ltd
9 Donnington Park, 85 Birdham Road, Chichester, West Sussex, PO20 7AJ
Order line: 01933 304 858

ISBN 978-1-83950-110-4

Printed and bound in Great Britain by Buxton Press Limited.

100 WINNERS

JUMPERS TO FOLLOW 2022-23

(ages as at 2022)

ADAMANTLY CHOSEN (IRE) 5 b g

Given Adamantly Chosen's pedigree is full of stamina – he's by Well Chosen out of a Shernazar mare with smart jumper Adamant Approach further down the dam's side – the 5yo has done well to win both a bumper and a maiden hurdle over 2m. He was stepped up in trip straight after that hurdle victory for his handicap debut and fared better than the bare result suggests when 11th of 23 in the Martin Pipe Conditional Jockeys' Handicap Hurdle at the Cheltenham Festival and he bettered that effort on his final start of last season at Punchestown (2m3f) in late April, making up plenty of ground in the last half mile to be nearest at the finish behind Camprond. He was sent off favourite for the Galway Hurdle on his first start of the new season in July and, although unable to figure over 2m, he left the impression he would make up into a good-quality handicapper over 2m4f and beyond and he's also bred to jump a fence in due course. WILLIE MULLINS

AHOY SENOR (IRE) 7 b g

If Ahoy Senor, who is by Dylan Thomas out of a mare who has produced a pair of stout stayers in Snuff Box and Daranova, can brush up his jumping, there's no reason why he won't be able to mix it with the best staying chasers around in the coming season. This highly regarded sort, who won a Grade 1 on only his second start over hurdles, was switched straight to fences last season and he was in the process of running a fine race in a traditionally strong Colin Parker Intermediate Chase when sprawling on landing and unseating his rider at the penultimate fence. He quickly made amends in a Newbury Grade 2 on Ladbrokes Trophy Day but the switch to both Grade 1 company and the sharper Kempton track found him out in the last half mile on Boxing Day when he made a series of errors and had to settle for second behind Bravemansgame. A bloodless victory in the Grade 2 Towton in February set him up nicely for a tilt at the Brown Advisory at the Cheltenham Festival and, given he made errors at a crucial stage, he deserves plenty of credit for getting as close to L'Homme Presse as he did. With both Bravemansgame and L'Homme Presse underperforming, he faced a fairly straightforward task to beat Fury Road in an Aintree Grade 1 on his final start in April, but he did it nicely from the front. This imposing sort has reportedly done well over the summer and his seasonal reappearance – possibly in the Charlie Hall at Wetherby – is eagerly awaited.
LUCINDA RUSSELL

ALAPHILIPPE (IRE) 8 b g

Fergal O'Brien's star is definitely in the ascendancy and last season's total of 128 winners and prize money totalling almost £1.38m was easily his best on both fronts since he took out a training licence. He joined forces with fellow Gloucestershire trainer Graeme McPherson from October 2021 and the partnership has plenty to look forward to this time round. One who could raise his game even higher is the already smart Alaphilippe, a Morozov half-brother to 2m4f chase winner Born For War, who confirmed that he retains all his ability despite a campaign that was restricted to just two starts. The 8yo shaped well after a break of 300 days in a Pertemps qualifier at Warwick in January and failed by only a neck to win the Pertemps itself at the Cheltenham Festival, in the process pulling a few lengths clear of the remainder. He's 4lb higher but, although he's the type to win again over hurdles, there's plenty of chase blood in his pedigree and it wouldn't be a surprise to see him go novice chasing this season. Whichever route he goes down, it will be a surprise if he doesn't win more races. FERGAL O'BRIEN

ALTOBELLI (IRE) 4 b g

Named after the striker who scored the third goal for Italy in the 1982 World Cup Final, which they won 3-1 against West Germany, Altobelli came in for significant market support when making his debut in an Exeter bumper in February. He duly ran out a comfortable winner from Ginny's Destiny, who would frank the form by winning his next start at Chepstow. Altobelli's trainer had not been sure that his charge would handle the soft underfoot conditions, so jockey Bryan Carver was instructed to give the 4yo a very patient ride and he carried out those tactics to perfection, bringing the gelding through late on to win without knowing he'd been in a race. Fry said afterwards: 'Although it wasn't the strongest bumper, you couldn't ask for a better debut and I will not be rushing him out again quickly.' It's possible that his initial target for this season will be a Class 1 bumper at Cheltenham in November, after which hurdling will be on the agenda. He has plenty of size and scope and he should become a useful jumper. HARRY FRY

AMERICAN MIKE (IRE) 5 b g

Such was the reputation of American Mike, backed up by the visual displays of effortless victories in a point and on his first two bumper starts in 2021, he started as the 5-2 second-favourite for the Champion Bumper at Cheltenham in March. This Mahler half-brother to 2m6f hurdle winner One Fine Man came unstuck that day behind the market leader and potential top-notcher Facile Vega, but he at least matched the form of his previous efforts and he showed a willing attitude in the closing stages. The 5yo took on Facile Vega and the rest of the Mullins battalions at Punchestown again but he ran as though feeling the effects of the Cheltenham race, finishing nearly 12l further behind that rival than on their meeting at Prestbury Park. However, he should be a different proposition in the coming season and he already looks a leading contender for the Ballymore, with the step up to 3m expected to suit if his pedigree is anything to go by. He remains a really exciting prospect. GORDON ELLIOTT

APPRECIATE IT (IRE) 8 b g

It was always going to be a big ask for Appreciate It to win the Champion Hurdle after exactly a year on the sidelines, but, despite not being able to justify odds of 100-30, he ran a good race, beaten by just over 9l by Honeysuckle, which was more than respectable in the circumstances. It may not have been the best Supreme Novices' Hurdle that he won in 2021, but it was hard not to be impressed with the way he won it and he is clearly built to be a chaser. That had been the plan until he had a setback earlier in the season, which tempted

Willie Mullins to keep him over hurdles and preserve his novice status over fences for this season. It's worth remembering that he was the 4-1 ante-post favourite for the Arkle prior to his setback and he's now 10-1 for the same race next season, and that looks a fair price. Providing he has a smoother preparation, he is surely capable of developing into a leading contender for that race this season. WILLIE MULLINS

ASHDALE BOB (IRE) 7 b g

An imposing gelding who also featured on these pages a year ago, Ashdale Bob must have broken a mirror at some point as he couldn't quite get his head in front throughout the season, despite running a string of good races. It all started in November when, while in the process of giving Bob Olinger and Bacardys a serious race, he blundered and unseated his rider three out when looking certain to be at least placed. He then ran another perfectly good race next time over 2m4f at Navan in early December but he couldn't quite get to Farouk D'Alene and Blue Sari. He admittedly had an off-day after that in late December, finishing last of seven finishers behind Fury Road in a Grade 1 Chase over 3m at Leopardstown, but he quickly bounced back to run another cracker back over hurdles at Gowran Park a month later, finishing third behind Royal Kahala and Home By The Lee in the Grade 2 Galmoy Hurdle, with Klassical Dream just behind him in fourth. On his next start in February he was headed on the line by Thedevilscoachman in another Grade 2 Hurdle at Navan before finishing an excellent third in the Coral Cup at Cheltenham behind shock winner Commander Of Fleet. His final start of the season was in the Grade 1 Champion Stayers' Hurdle at Punchestown, where he finished 1¼l behind a revitalised Klassical Dream, with the likes of Gentlemansgame, Sire Du Berlais, Paisley Park and Concertista all in behind. He's essentially an out-and-out stayer on the evidence of those runs and hopefully he can be found suitable opportunities over the winter to finally break his losing run. It would be no surprise to see him line up in the Stayers' Hurdle in March and he'd have a decent each-way chance in that based on what we saw of him last season. JESSICA HARRINGTON

AUTUMN RETURN (IRE) 5 b m

Ruth Jefferson has had mixed fortunes since taking the trainer's licence from her late father Malcolm, but she's a most capable operator who, like the name of her former Grade 1 winner Waiting Patiently, always gives her horses plenty of time. Sold for £55,000 after winning an Irish point on her third start, Autumn Return, a Fame And Glory half-sister to useful 2m-2m5f hurdle winner Ferrobin and 2m1f chase winner Minella Hub, was prominent in the market and showed a determined attitude to win a traditionally strong Ayr bumper on her debut under Rules and on her first start for Jefferson in April this year. The bare form of that renewal doesn't look anything out of the ordinary, but the 5yo should benefit from a step up in trip when she goes over hurdles this season, and there's enough in her pedigree to suggest she'll jump a fence further down the line. She's open to plenty of improvement and can win away from the better types in novice company before going on to ply her trade in handicaps. RUTH JEFFERSON

AUTHORISED SPEED (FR) 5 b g

Although his record reads one win from five starts in bumpers, this half-brother to a couple of winners on the Flat and over hurdles in France (out of a French middle-distance winner) was one of the better performers around in that sphere and he's a good prospect for hurdles this term. Word was out that he had plenty of ability as he started at 6-5 favourite for his debut run at Market Rasen last May and, although unable to justify his position at the head of the market behind Grozni, he showed more than enough after being hampered to suggest that he'd win a race. His reputation was enhanced in Listed company at Ascot on his next outing seven months later before he bolted up (beating a Paul Nicholls newcomer and an Alan King previous winner) by upwards of 10l in January. The 5yo ran to a similar Raceform rating back in Listed company and back at Newbury just over three weeks later before finishing fifth in the Champion Bumper behind Facile Vega and American Mike, faring best of the British contingent. There's jumping winners in his pedigree and he's the type to do well in this new discipline. We look forward to seeing him again. GARY MOORE

BALCO COASTAL (FR) 6 b g

A disappointing favourite for the Grade 2 bumper at the 2021 Aintree festival, Balco Coastal put his career back on track by winning by 6l on his hurdling debut at Huntingdon in December. That race, over 2m, has already worked out well and Balco Coastal did his bit for the form by defying his penalty in workmanlike fashion at Ludlow at the end of the same month. He then finished a good second (with the hood left off) behind North Lodge in a Grade 2 over 2m4f at Cheltenham at the end of January, but the suspicion was that he didn't quite see out the longer trip. He was sent off favourite for the Imperial Cup at Sandown on the back of that run, but he weakened quickly from two out and was soon pulled up, with his trainer confirming afterwards that the soft ground at Sandown didn't suit his charge at all. He bounced back to form on good-to-soft ground at Aintree in a Grade 3 handicap over

2m4f, where he finished third behind Langer Dan and Fils D'oudairies. He didn't enjoy the clearest of passages from the second-last, but he probably wouldn't have finished better than third in any case. Perhaps 2m4f stretched his stamina again, so, in the circumstances, it was a satisfactory effort and it proved his Sandown running to be all wrong. He's been dropped a pound by the handicapper after that third place and there's still mileage in his new handicap mark of 133 over hurdles but, as a former Irish pointer, he may soon be switched to fences and it's easy to see him rating a little bit higher in that discipline. NICKY HENDERSON

BALLYGRIFINCOTTAGE (IRE) 7 b g

The Bristol Novices' Hurdle, which was run at Cheltenham in mid-December and won by Blazing Khal, has worked out well with the runner-up Gelino Bello winning the Grade 1 Sefton Novices' Hurdle three starts later in April, while the third, fourth and fifth all won races subsequently. The only horse making his Rules debut that day was Ballygrifincottage, and he outran his odds of 22-1 as he finished just over 6l behind the winner in third, having led as they approached the final obstacle. This three-time point winner duly confirmed the promise of that initial outing by comfortably beating High Stakes, a subsequent winner, over 2m7f at Lingfield in January. That was on heavy ground but he had no problems with much faster conditions at the Cheltenham Festival as he fared best of the British contingent in the Grade 1 Albert Bartlett Novices' Hurdle, ultimately finishing fourth behind The Nice Guy, Minella Cocooner and Bardenstown Lad. Harry Skelton had trotted out the 'whatever he achieves over hurdles is a bonus' line after his Lingfield win, which augurs well for what now lies ahead. Clearly he's not ground dependent so we can expect to see him in novice chases at around 3m in the autumn. Perhaps a return trip to Cheltenham in March is already being mapped out for him – he's currently 33-1 for the Brown Advisory Novices' Chase on the Wednesday, but he may also be worth a second glance in the National Hunt Chase on the opening day, for which he is currently 25-1. DAN SKELTON

BARDENSTOWN LAD 7 ch g

John McConnell, who is a qualified vet, began training racehorses in 2001, although it took him four years to get off the mark. He now supplies a steady stream of winners from his County Meath base where he has been for about a decade. One of his rising stars last season was Bardenstown Lad, a bumper winner in March 2021 who won four of his first five hurdles starts between July of that year and February 2022. Having won a maiden hurdle over 3m at Wexford in July and a novice hurdle over 2m6f at Cartmel in August, he simply found 2m5f 170y at Navan an insufficient test of stamina as he finished a close third behind Tullybeg and Edison Kent in September. He was then stepped up to 3m at Cheltenham in October and got the better of Dragon Bones, running out a determined winner, which is always a good trait in a stayer. He probably didn't have to improve on that when following up in a three-runner novice under a penalty at Musselburgh in February. However, his next start at Cheltenham in the Albert Bartlett Novices' Hurdle produced a career best as he finished third behind The Nice Guy and Minella Cocooner, staying on stoutly once again without ever looking likely to lay a glove on the two classier horses who finished ahead of him. Afterwards, a representative for the trainer said: 'We're delighted with the run. The ground was probably a bit slow for Bardenstown Lad, but he's a big chaser in the making.' He took on the first two in the Albert Bartlett again at Punchestown in another Grade 1 but his race ended early as he fell at the second. He's certainly one to look forward to as he now embarks on his chasing career and, given that he's unlikely to beat The Nice Guy Or Minella Cocooner in the Brown Advisory Novices' Chase at Cheltenham, he may be worth siding with in the National Hunt Chase, for which he is a general 20-1. JOHN MCCONNELL

BEAUPORT (IRE) 6 b g

Although Beauport, the first foal of a close relation to a 2m4f-2m6f hurdle and chase winner Oscar Barton, won only one of his five starts over hurdles last season, he quickly made up into a smart performer and he's the type who could raise his game if he goes down the novice chasing route this season. This well-built 6yo, who is certainly bred to jump a fence, improved steadily throughout last season and his best run came when he scored over 2m4f at Uttoxeter on Midlands National Day in March, form that was franked by the subsequent win of the third Panic Attack. Although he couldn't build on that effort from a 6lb higher mark over 3m 149y, the longest trip he's tackled, at Aintree in April on his final outing of the season, he ran a bit better than the bare facts suggest after meeting a bit of trouble turning for home. He has age on his side, he's in very good hands and he's sure to win more races. NIGEL TWISTON-DAVIES

BLAZING KHAL (IRE) 6 b g

After Blazing Khal won his first three starts over hurdles, including two Grade 2s at Cheltenham over 2m5f and 3m in November and December, trainer Charles Byrnes was already making comparisons with his previous Cheltenham Festival winner Weapon's Amnesty, who won the Albert Bartlett Novices' Hurdle in 2009 before returning to the scene of his victory a year later to add the Grade 1 RSA Chase. Following his bloodless win in the Grade 2 Bristol Novices' Hurdle in mid-December, Blazing Khal was chalked up as the 4-1 favourite for last season's Albert Bartlett and he had been expected to contest a Grade 1 at the Dublin Racing Festival in February beforehand. However, in late January it was announced that the gelding had suffered a minor setback and that he would therefore miss both Leopardstown and Cheltenham, although the trainer was at that stage planning a comeback at the Punchestown Festival in late April. That comeback run didn't materialise however, so it is hoped that the extended time off has allowed the 6yo to make a full recovery. He is now likely to be switched to fences and, given what Weapon's Amnesty achieved, it would be foolish to underestimate him at 20-1 for the Brown Advisory Novices' Chase (formerly the RSA Chase). CHARLES BYRNES

BOOMBAWN (IRE) 5 b g

Dan Skelton is now firmly established in the upper echelons of the training ranks, having finished in the top three in the jumps trainers' championship for each of the last four seasons and earning more than £2m in total prize money for the first time last season. His Boombawn, by Dylan Thomas out of a dam who has several French jump winners in her pedigree, looks a likely candidate to add to the yard's prize money this time around judged on his performances as a novice hurdler last season. His two wins at Southwell and Ffos Las (on good, made all both times) at prohibitive odds didn't tell us much about him, but the 5yo looks the type to win races in handicap company judged on his final effort of the season at Sandown when chasing home Knappers Hill, an unbeaten bumper horse who was notching his fourth victory over hurdles. Boombawn starts the current campaign on an official rating of 122, which should afford him plenty of winnable opportunities and his pedigree suggests he'll stay further. DAN SKELTON

BRIDGE NORTH (IRE) 6 b g

Fourth in an Irish point in April 2021, Bridge North looked in need of the experience on his first two starts over hurdles over 2m5f at Ludlow in November and at Sedgefield over 2m4f in early December, but he made rapid strides from that point onward. First, he finished a staying-on second behind Green Book, a future Grade 3 winner, at Ludlow in a handicap over 2m5f and the following month he went one better over that same C&D when edging out Phantom Getaway, with a couple of future winners well beaten off. Stepped up to 3m, he was pulled up in the River Don Novices' Hurdle at Doncaster at the end of January, but it was reported that he had made a respiratory noise and he was given wind surgery. He made a winning return from that break in a three-runner novice at Bangor in March, pulling right away from Silver Flyer over 2m3f 123y, which would have already been the bare minimum for him. He was stepped up in trip and class on his final start and finished a respectable fifth of 14 at odds of 80-1 behind Gelino Bello in the Grade 1 Sefton Novices' Hurdle over 3m 149y, where he was noted as staying on better than many. It's likely that he will now be switched to fences and, given his upward trajectory over hurdles, he should soon be winning races, particularly as he starts tackling staying trips. HENRY DALY

BRING ON THE NIGHT 5 ch g

Before Bring On The Night next runs over hurdles, he may take up an engagement in the Group 1 Irish St Leger at the Curragh in September. This dual

French Flat winner, who also has plenty of French Flat winners in his pedigree, won easily on his hurdles debut and first run for the yard after an absence at Naas in February but, as was the case with all the beaten horses, he was made to look pedestrian behind Constitution Hill in the Supreme Novices' Hurdle at Cheltenham in March. The 5yo looked to have decent prospects for his final hurdle run at Punchestown, but he wasn't at his very best, despite dropping down in class, ultimately finishing fifth behind El Fabiolo. He ran a fine race back on the Flat when touched off by subsequent easy winner Coltrane at Royal Ascot (2m4f), but he'll need a big step forward to give himself any chance in the Irish St Leger and he looks more a Cesarewitch type, a race which his trainer has won three times in the last four seasons. Whatever happens on the Flat, he's one to look out for when he goes back over hurdles and presumably when he steps up to 2m4f or beyond. There's a decent handicap in him before he goes up in grade. WILLIE MULLINS

CALL OF THE WILD (IRE) 5 b g

The wide-margin winner of a Huntingdon bumper in May 2021 which has worked out well, this half brother to stablemate Chatez was touched off by Onemorefortheroad on his hurdles bow at Stratford in October, but he probably would have won had he not got the last flight all wrong. The pair had pulled a mile clear of the rest and the winner went on to win his next two starts so it was a decent effort all in all. Call Of The Wild made no mistake next time at Kempton in November, getting the better of Petrossian in a three-runner novice hurdle over 2m. He was next seen at Doncaster in March where he comfortably beat Boombawn on heavy ground over 2m 128y and that rival franked the form by winning his next two. He couldn't complete the hat-trick at Cheltenham over 2m4f in April, but he still ran a great race behind Pull Again Green and Royaume Uni, who both brought a decent level of form to the table. It also appeared that the longer trip and the uphill finish was just too stiff for him. He appeals as a handicap hurdler to follow over slightly shorter distances with an official rating of 130 looking very manageable. ALAN KING

CATCH THE SWALLOWS (IRE) 8 b g

Having finished just 1½l behind Appreciate It in an Irish point in March 2018, Catch The Swallows made a winning debut in a Bangor bumper for David Pipe in January 2019, beating the Venetia Williams-trained Frenchy Du Large, who is now established as a decent handicap chaser. He wasn't seen again for nearly three years after that initial run, but he made his comeback for a new trainer, the aforementioned Venetia Williams, in a Leicester maiden hurdle last December. He ran a creditable race too, finishing a close third behind Sholokjack and Let's Have Another, who would both go on to win again. Catch The Swallows wasn't seen again after that, which is an obvious worry, but his trainer confirmed in August that he was on course to return to the track and hopefully he can quickly pick up the winning thread. He may have a run or two over hurdles first but the plan is to switch him to fences sooner rather than later. He's still only eight and, while he's a risky proposition for this list given his veterinary history, he could easily run up a sequence once he resumes his career. VENETIA WILLIAMS

CHAMPAGNE TOWN 5 b g

A £180,000 purchase after winning a point at Kirkistown in November 2021, Champagne Town made his debut in a Leopardstown bumper in March and he ran a promising race, making the best of his way home from the home turn before being headed by a Willie Mullins-trained hotpot about a furlong out and then losing second place close home. A month later he finished third again, this time in an 18-runner maiden hurdle at Limerick, which was a fair effort, especially when you consider that he could have jumped better. He will surely improve in that department and he's in the right hands to turn into a decent handicapper as he gains more experience. GAVIN CROMWELL

CHANGING THE RULES (IRE) 5 b g

Owned by JP McManus and from the same family as Moscow Flyer, Changing The Rules has a fair bit to live up to, but he made a decent start to his career in three maiden hurdles in the early part of this year, which offers plenty of hope for the future. He looked very much in need of the experience on the first occasion at Fairyhouse in January as he finished a well-beaten fourth of 12 over 2m4f, losing touch with the leaders after a mid-race forward move. He improved markedly on that when finishing fifth of 18 behind Bring On The Night in a better race over 2m at Naas in February, with the slower ground appearing to suit him well. He then ran a very similar race back at Fairyhouse on his final start in April, where he was only beaten 6¾l by the winner Whatsavailable, having been badly hampered by a faller two out, which cost him at least a couple of lengths. There's further scope for progress as he gains more experience and there looks to be mileage in his mark of 116 for him in handicaps. JESSICA HARRINGTON

CITY CHIEF (IRE) 5 b g

The Soldier Of Fortune gelding, who cost a not-inconsiderable £210,000 at Cheltenham just over a year ago after winning an Irish point, has a stack of stamina in his pedigree and, following promising efforts over slightly shorter at Ascot and at Doncaster on his first two starts for Nicky Henderson, he didn't have to improve to get off the mark upped to 3m1f 119y at Hereford in March. He quickly left that form behind on his handicap debut at Ayr when he followed up to beat subsequent winner Hidden Heroics over 3m, with the pair clear of the remainder. However, his best effort was saved for his latest start at Punchestown when he plugged on to a gritty fifth of 20 finishers behind A Great View, in a race that has thrown up subsequent Flat, hurdle and even chase winners. It may well be that his trainer elects to send him over fences sooner rather than later. Whatever path he goes down, the 5yo is a likeable sort who is sure to win more races granted a suitable test of stamina. NICKY HENDERSON

COBBLERS DREAM (IRE) 6 br g

Trainer Ben Case and conditional jockey Jack Andrews had a day to remember at Doncaster last December, the pair combining to land a quickfire double with The Golden Rebel in the handicap chase and Cobblers Dream in the 2m3f handicap hurdle. And, although Jack Quinlan replaced Andrews in the valuable and prestigious Lanzarote Handicap Hurdle at Kempton just over a month later, the 6yo cemented himself as a firmly progressive sort when going clear in the closing stages to beat Highway One O Two by just over 5l, with several subsequent winners down the field. He was put away for a couple of months afterwards before repeating that form reunited with Andrews in the Martin Pipe, even though he was unable to fend off Joseph O'Brien's Banbridge in the closing stages. However, he beat everything else comprehensively enough. He ran poorly on his next start at Aintree, a wide trip not helping but certainly not the contributory factor to his defeat. It's best to put a line through that run and start afresh this season. At this stage it's not clear whether he'll stay hurdling or go chasing – there's certainly enough chase blood in his pedigree to think he'll do well over fences when the time comes. BEN CASE

CONSTITUTION HILL 5 b g

Hands up! Did anyone think Jonbon would run his race and still be beaten by 22l at level weights at the Cheltenham Festival? Nor did we, but that's exactly how it turned out with the Nicky Henderson runner put firmly in his place by impressive winner and stable companion Constitution Hill in the Supreme Novices' Hurdle - the opening race on Tuesday. But, back to the beginning. Constitution Hill, the first foal of a 2m–2m2f hurdle winner, was beaten in an Irish point on debut last April – the winner, Anyharminasking, went on to win twice over hurdles for Jonjo O'Neill in the latest season – but he showed enough to see him make £120,000 at the sales the following month. He showed he was a bit special when bolting up at Sandown on his Rules debut before following up in impressive fashion in the Grade 1 Tolworth Hurdle at the same course in January. But he produced that 'wow' moment at Cheltenham when powering clear in the straight to win eased down by almost a distance in course record time in the Supreme – a performance that would have made him very hard to beat had he contested the Champion Hurdle (run almost six seconds slower) over the same course and distance two hours later. After the race his trainer said: 'Constitution Hill must be an extraordinary animal. This is a very, very good horse. Jonbon is a very good horse and for him to do that to him is remarkable. He's got an enormous turn of foot, he's always just racing two gears below everybody else because it's all so easy for him.

Aintree comes very quickly; he could go to Punchestown and we'll say hello to Willie [Mullins] again and see what happens.' Aintree, as expected, passed him by, but he also sidestepped Punchestown and he now goes into the new season as the 7-4 favourite for this season's Champion Hurdle. After only three runs over hurdles, it's scary to think there's almost certainly more to come and it's to be hoped nothing prevents him from developing into the best hurdler we've seen in a very long time.

NICKY HENDERSON

CORACH RAMBLER (IRE) 8 b g

Knowing what we know now about Corach Rambler, it's a bit of a mystery how he took five starts to win a race in the point-to-point sphere. But, it's been an upward curve ever since that victory and, after winning two of his three hurdles starts for Lucinda Russell, his form has gone to a different level over fences. That wasn't totally unexpected given his pedigree (his dam is a half-sister to very useful chase winner A Glass In Thyne out of a half-sister to high-class jumper Native Upmanship) and, following wins at Aintree and Cheltenham in the last half of 2021, he turned in his best effort when winning the Ultima Handicap Chase over 3m1f at the Cheltenham Festival. On that occasion he made up a considerable amount of ground in the last half mile before taking the lead in the closing stage to triumph in a typically competitive event. There was talk he'd be an ideal type for the bet365 at Sandown, but he sidestepped that due to the quick ground and he also missed Punchestown. The 8yo is the type to do even better this year and, although at this stage he looks like an ideal Grand National sort – a race his yard won in 2017 with One For Arthur – he could make up into a solid graded horse granted further progress. His yard has been seen to really good effect with staying chasers and he's very much one to keep on the right side this season. He's effective on a range of going from good to heavy. LUCINDA RUSSELL

CRYSTAL GLORY 6 b g

Crystal Glory quickly made up into a very useful staying hurdler last season but it's over fences that he's likely to fulfil his considerable potential, especially if his pedigree is anything to go by. The Fame And Glory 6yo made 95,000 euros on the back of winning both his starts in Irish points in 2020 and he recouped a chunk of that investment in his first season over hurdles, winning twice and finishing placed twice in Graded company, firstly when chasing home the promising Hillcrest in a Grade 2 at Haydock on heavy ground and then when fourth to Gelino Bello in the Grade 1 Sefton Novices' Hurdle (3m) on his final outing in April. Trainer Nicky Richards tends to bring his horses along steadily so don't expect him to be overfaced in the early part of the season, assuming he goes down the novice chase route. Tracks like Ayr or Carlisle are likely to be in the thinking, he's sure to have been well schooled and it'll be a surprise if he doesn't make an impact. He's only raced on good to soft and softer ground and he stays 3m well. NICKY RICHARDS

DALAMOI (IRE) 5 b g

A half-brother to six winners, most notably Don Poli who won the RSA Chase for Willie Mullins in 2015, Dalamoi had shown promise in two bumpers in April and October 2021 and he made a pleasing start to his hurdling career at Ffos Las in November as he won a 2m contest on soft ground from Port Or Starboard and Greenrock Abbey. He ran another sound race under a penalty over 2m4f at the same course the following month, but he wasn't quite able to concede 7lb to Bowtogreatness, who would frank the form by winning his next start by 8½l.

He acquitted himself well again on his third start in a novices' handicap hurdle over 2m4f at Sandown in March, finishing third of eight behind Bourbali, who would go on to win his next two, and Dom Of Mary, who also won next time out. He was able to run off the same mark at Warwick over 2m3f in April and on the face of it he was a bit disappointing as he trailed in fifth of 11 behind Ashoka. However, that race was run on the fastest ground he'd encountered to date and it clearly didn't suit him as he got outpaced by the principals at a crucial stage. The handicapper has dropped him 2lb for that run and he should be able to take full advantage when he gets his optimum conditions again. He's a long-term chasing prospect but he can make his mark in handicap hurdles first.
TIM VAUGHAN

DINOBLUE (FR) 5 ch m

Dinoblue is a 5yo half-sister to bumper/2m4f hurdle/chase winner Blue Sari out of a French 2m1f chase winning half-sister from the family of smart 2m–3m1f hurdle/chase winner/Grand National second Royal Auclair and she did her bit for the pedigree when winning on her debut at Clonmel in January, jumping well and asserting in the last quarter mile to pull clear of La Prima Donna and Mi Lighthouse, both of whom have since won over hurdles. A step up in grade was always going to be the way forward after that impressive run and, although she didn't manage to win again, she ran respectably after being upped to 2m4f in a Grade 1 at Fairyhouse in April and then when returned to 2m in a Listed event at Punchestown on her final start. She shaped on that last outing as though the return to 2m4f would be more to her liking, she has age on her side and an official rating of 134 (in Ireland) gives her a chance if and when she dips her toe into the handicap sphere. WILLIE MULLINS

DUBROVNIK HARRY (IRE) 6 b g

This half-brother to useful 2m hurdle winner Knockmaole Boy was notably green on his first-ever hurdles start over 2m at Exeter in December, but he still ran a cracker against more experienced rivals to finish third of 18 behind Hermes Boy and American Gerry, with the fourth home nearly 10l further back. Four weeks later he turned the tables on the runner-up in emphatic fashion at the same track as he put clear daylight between himself and that rival over 18.5f on heavy ground. A further step up in trip at Leicester in February didn't quite pay dividends as he was touched off by Anglers Crag, with the 6lb penalty he carried for his Exeter win making the difference between victory and defeat. Given a mark of 125 after that, he made his handicap debut in a hot Grade 3 contest at Sandown in March, where he ran an excellent race to finish third behind Complete Unknown and Marble Sands over 2m4f (soft), doing best of the horses who came from off the pace. He wasn't seen again after that run but he has scope for further progress and he can quickly make his mark in handicaps at around 2m4f on soft or heavy ground, with an official rating of 127 looking very fair. In the long term, he will make a lovely chaser. HARRY FRY

DUSART (IRE) 7 b g

Nicky Henderson knows exactly what it takes to win the Ladbrokes Trophy at Newbury (on 26 November this year) having won the race this century with Trabolgan in 2005, with subsequent Cheltenham Gold Cup winner Bobs Worth in 2012 and with Triolo

D'Alene the following year. And the master of Seven Barrows looks to have another likely candidate for the race in the shape of Dusart, who quickly made up into a smart novice chaser in the latest season. This Flemensfirth half-brother to high-class former stable companion Simonsig only had two outings over hurdles, but he was placed in Grade 1 company on the second of those and he only needed to match that level of form to win his first two starts over fences at Leicester and at Exeter. He was pitched in with the big boys in the Brown Advisory Novices' Chase and, although he had his limitations exposed to an extent, he was far from disgraced in a race that threw up subsequent Grade 1 winners Ahoy Senor (second) and Capodanno (fourth). However, he reserved his best effort for his handicap debut on Scottish Grand National Day at Ayr when grinding it out to beat Sounds Russian, the pair pulling clear of the remainder. The 7yo is suited by a decent test of stamina, there's room for improvement in the jumping department and the Ladbrokes Trophy should be a good gauge of whether he'll be able to hold his own back in Graded company. He's 10-1 for the Newbury race at the time of writing and that looks pretty good value. NICKY HENDERSON

EDITEUR DU GITE (FR) 8 b g

The winner of four of his last seven starts, Editeur Du Gite may still be improving at the age of eight and he is one to keep in mind for this season's Grand Annual provided it does not come up soft or heavy at Cheltenham in March. He also ran in that race in 2022, finishing an excellent fourth behind Global Citizen, only giving way late on the heavy ground, which would not have suited him at all. All of his previous wins had come on good to soft or quicker and he has also never won beyond the bare two miles, which goes a long way to explaining his defeat in the Melling Chase at Aintree in April, which is run over 2m4f. The previous season he had won the Red Rum Chase over 2m at the same meeting, so it was somewhat surprising to see him tackle the longer trip. He will remain a force over the minimum distance and presumably the Grand Annual will firmly be on the agenda again this season, particularly when you consider his excellent course record at Cheltenham – his previous two visits before last season's Grand Annual fourth yielded two wins. GARY MOORE

EDWARDSTONE 8 b g

Alan King is renowned for being patient with his horses but even that must have been tested to the limit given the trainer's losing run at the Cheltenham Festival that stretched back to 2015 going into last season's showpiece. However, the planets aligned and the losing run was broken courtesy of Edwardstone's fluent victory in the Arkle chase. And it had been a pretty straightforward path to get to Cheltenham, the only blip on his chase record when brought down at Warwick on his reappearance last November. He made amends in novice company back at that course on his next start and took the jump into Grade 1 company in his stride when winning the Henry VIII at Sandown on Tingle Creek day in early December. Grade 2 wins followed at Kempton and Warwick – his sound jumping a feature of those victories – and, after a bit of an early scare when a rival fell in front of him in the Arkle, he appreciated the strong gallop and he powered clear in the closing stages to win by just over 4l from Gabynako. As a result he was made odds-on to extend his winning run at Aintree on his final start, but he couldn't get to grips with Gentleman De Mee, who was given the perfect front-running ride at a track that suits those tactics. Nonetheless, the 8yo ran close to his best form and, although he'll face tougher opposition in a strong 2m division this time round, his jumping should continue to stand him in good stead and his stamina-laden pedigree suggests he'll be just as effective over further. ALAN KING

EL FABIOLO (FR) 5 b g

El Fabiolo showed a fair bit when placed in a Listed Hurdle in France on his hurdling debut in September 2020 (in a race for those who hadn't raced over jumps) but he's turned into a far superior animal than those who beat him thanks to his exploits for multiple Irish champion trainer Willie Mullins. Nobody was going to get rich backing him at 2-7 for his first run for the yard at Tramore on New Year's Day, but he duly bolted up, in the process beating subsequent winners Tempo Chapter Two and Hide And Seek by 13l and just over 22l respectively. He sidestepped Cheltenham due to an injury picked up before the Dublin Festival but stepped up considerably on the Tramore run when pitched into a Grade 1 at Aintree on his next start in April in a first-time hood. He may well have beaten Nicky Henderson's Jonbon had he not been hampered early in the home straight and had he jumped the last cleanly so, in the circumstances that effort can be marked up a touch. He faced a straightforward task returned to non-Graded competition on his final start at Punchestown in April and he didn't have to improve to justify his position at the head of the market. After the Aintree run, Mullins suggested that he was looking forward to going down the novice chase route (there's plenty of chase blood in his pedigree) and, after only five career outings, it's fairly safe to assume there's more improvement to come. Time will reveal his position in the pecking order at a yard that's usually full of talent in the novice chasing department but, at this stage, the 5yo is a most exciting prospect and one who should stay a fair bit further than two miles and two furlongs – the longest trip he's tackled to date over hurdles. WILLIE MULLINS

ENERGUMENE (FR) 8 br g

By far the best finish of the 2021-22 jumps season was the Clarence House Chase at Ascot in January where we finally witnessed the eagerly anticipated clash between Shishkin and Energumene, with both of them putting their unbeaten chase records on the line. Such clashes can often end in anti-climax, but this one turned into a tussle for the ages, with Energumene leading from the off and appearing to have his rival's measure as they came to the last, only to be worn down in the last 100 yards. Just 1l separated them at the finish and the rematch at Cheltenham in the Queen Mother Champion Chase was being anticipated with great excitement. That race, however, did end in disappointment as Shishkin looked a shadow of himself throughout and was eventually pulled up on the heavy ground, while the third favourite Chacun Pour Soi unseated his rider at the fifth-last. That left Energumene with a proverbial penalty kick and he converted the opportunity with ease, beating Funambule Sivola and Envoi Allen with plenty left in the tank. He ran to a similar level at Punchestown the following month, beating Chacun Pour Soi and Envoi Allen in a tactical battle for the Grade 1 Champion Chase, his fourth win at the highest level. Clearly the best 2m chaser in Ireland and still only eight, it can only be hoped that the 'real' Shishkin shows up at Cheltenham next March and we get a similar contest to the one we witnessed at Ascot in January. WILLIE MULLINS

ERNE RIVER (IRE) 7 b g

A dual hurdles winner in the spring of 2021, Erne River took the notable scalp of Beakstown when winning a novices' handicap chase at Doncaster in January, with the likes of Champagnesuperover, Gallyhill and Our Power, all future chase winners, among the beaten horses. His next assignment in February was a 2m5f novices' chase at Wetherby where he beat a reliable yardstick in the shape of Uncle Alistair by 13l, with Champagnesuperover further behind again. Although his jumping could have been better, he looked a proper galloper who will no doubt benefit from the step up to around 3m in time. His trainer was delighted with him, saying: 'He oozes chasing and I was really pleased with that.' His next run came at the Grand National meeting at Aintree, where he was upped into Grade 1 company for the first time as he contested the Manifesto Novices' Chase over 2m4f. He was still in there pitching when he was unsighted and took a fall at the tenth, although of course it was far too early to know for sure how he would have fared. His final run was in a strong Grade 2 at Sandown on the final day of the jumps season, where he showed up well for a long way before having to give best to Saint Calvados and Mister Fisher, who are both rated about a stone higher than him. There are more races to be won with this Irish maiden point winner, especially if his sights are lowered slightly, and it will be no surprise to see him stepping up to 3m before too long. NICK KENT

FACILE VEGA (IRE) 5 b g

Overstating things is a common occurrence with racing observers and commentators but there really is a chance that Facile Vega could be an outstanding jumps performer judged on both pedigree and an unbeaten bumper career that spanned four races and produced as many wins – including two at the highest level. He is bred to be special, being out of an outstanding racemare in Quevega – who won the mares' hurdle at Cheltenham a staggering six times – though the first foal of the dam turned out to be nothing out of the ordinary. The 5yo shot to the head of the Champion bumper market at the Cheltenham Festival following an impressive debut at Leopardstown on Boxing Day before taking the step up to Grade 2 company in his stride on his next outing at the Dublin Festival in February, travelling strongly throughout before powering clear to win by 12l, a race that teed him up perfectly for a tilt at Cheltenham. And the 5yo didn't disappoint at Prestbury Park the following month, responding well to pressure to beat main market rival American Mike, who had also created a good impression in bumpers, in fine style. With that rival slightly below his best at Punchestown, Facile Vega didn't have to improve to extend his unbeaten record but he also showed a different side in that he battled on tenaciously under pressure to get the better of stable companion Redemption Day. After Cheltenham, trainer Willie Mullins said: 'Facile Vega looks the real deal as we always thought. These conditions weren't conducive for him to produce his best but he still did the business. I've compared him to Florida Pearl, who was a very good bumper horse, and that's how highly we regard him. He'd be in the top percentage of our winners of this race. He's very easy to train and we just keep a lid on him all the time. He could stay at this trip or go over further, but we'll think about that once he's won a maiden hurdle. I don't know how good he is – he covers an awful lot of ground when he's galloping and he has plenty of speed.' High praise indeed from one who has dealt with some of the best National Hunt horses in training in the last two decades and, although his price is likely to be prohibitive when he makes his debut over hurdles, he'll be one of the main draws of the new season. WILLIE MULLINS

FERNY HOLLOW (IRE) 7 bb g

The red-hot favourite for this year's Arkle, Ferny Hollow was ruled out for the season in late January because of a suspensory ligament injury. It appears not to have been a serious setback, however, with Willie Mullins saying at the time: 'He came home very sore from Leopardstown and we were just hoping he might have got away with it. He did his first canter during the week and, unfortunately, he's sore again after it. We've decided to pull up stumps for the whole season, rather than trying to get him back for Punchestown.' Before that news, the 2020 Champion Bumper winner hadn't been seen for just over a year when comfortably winning a 2m1f beginners' chase at Punchestown in early December, with Coeur Sublime, Thedevilscoachman, You Raised Me Up and Gentlemen De Mee the next four home. Next, he had to concede 13lb to smart mare Riviere D'Etel in the Grade 1 *Racing Post* Novice Chase at Leopardstown on St. Stephen's Day, but he was equal to the task as he ran out a determined winner. Sadly, that was the last we saw of him, but a horse with that much class should certainly not be forgotten. We are all eagerly anticipating another clash between a fully fit Shishkin and Energumene in this season's Queen Mother Champion Chase, but how about if we add Ferny Hollow to that mix? Now that would be a race to savour! He's a general 8-1 at the time of writing and he's probably slightly below Energumene in the pecking order at Closutton, but it is definitely a clash that would quicken the pulse if it were to happen. WILLIE MULLINS

FIL DOR (FR) 4 gr g

If Vauban hadn't been around, it's not inconceivable that Fil Dor could have been unbeaten in six starts in his first season over hurdles. After a promising Flat run in France, after which he was picked up for 88,000 euros, he made an immediate impact over hurdles for new connections, beating a host of subsequent winners at Down Royal in late October. Grade 3 and Grade 2 victories soon followed at Fairyhouse in November and Leopardstown on Boxing Day, the manner of those wins suggesting strongly that he was a valid Triumph Hurdle candidate. However, his three runs in Grade 1 company at the Dublin, Cheltenham and Punchestown Festivals saw him finish second – a similar distance beaten on each occasion – to the Mullins-trained Vauban. While the 4yo may not reverse placings with his old rival over 2m, there's a good chance that he can take his form to a higher level as he goes up in trip judged both on his pedigree and the fact that his trainer kept referring to him as a relaxed individual after his three wins. He's a half-brother to a 2m6f chase winner out of a dam who is an unraced half-sister to Cheltenham Gold Cup scorer A Plus Tard so expect to see some improvement when he's upped to 2m4f or beyond in the coming season. The son of Doctor Dino is open to plenty of improvement and it could be worth exploiting his current Irish handicap mark of 146 before he goes back into Graded company.
GORDON ELLIOTT

FIRST STREET 5 b g

A half-brother to 1m2f AW winner To The Moon and 1m 2yo winner Pioneer Spirit, First Street had shown a decent level of ability in two bumpers in the summer of 2021 and he didn't have to improve much on those runs to get off the mark at the first time of asking over hurdles at Bangor in mid-August. He pulled a mile clear with the Donald McCain-trained Zafar and that horse went on to frank the form next time by winning a similar race at Kelso. First Street had no problem following up his win under a penalty at Warwick in September, beating The Brimming Water with ease over 2m5f. Next he was stepped up to Grade 2 company at Chepstow in October as he contested the Persian War Novices' Hurdle over 2m3f 100y, but he raced very keenly before weakening in the straight to finish a well-beaten fifth behind Camprond. Given wind surgery after that run, he bounced back to winning form at Kempton over 2m in January, winning a Class 3 handicap off an official mark of 132. The handicapper put him up 9lb and, although he ran a fine race, he had to settle for third behind Glory And Fortune and I Like To Move It in the Betfair Hurdle at Newbury in February. He was put up another 1lb for that, but he ran a career-best next time when finishing second to the classy State Man in the County Hurdle at the Cheltenham Festival, with the winner going on to win a Grade 1 next time. First Street was also pitched into a Grade 1 on his next outing but he was found wanting behind stablemate Jonbon in the Top Novices' Hurdle at Aintree, finishing a well-beaten fifth of nine. In hindsight it was probably a mistake to run him as he looked a little flat and Nicky Henderson had originally intended to draw stumps on his season after his excellent County Hurdle run. Forgive him that Aintree effort and he still has a very progressive profile and, still only five, he should be capable of winning more races. NICKY HENDERSON

FLOORING PORTER (IRE) 7 b g

In March, Flooring Porter joined the likes of Big Buck's, Inglis Drever and Baracouda, all of whom had

won the Stayers' Hurdle at the Cheltenham Festival more than once this century. And, while he needs to raise his game again in terms of official ratings to rank alongside those top-class performers, another victory in that Grade 1 event will put him alongside Howard Johnson's Inglis Drever, who lifted the prize in 2005, 2007 and 2008. A season that was restricted to just four runs brought a fall over an inadequate 2m4f on reappearance, but he showed that all his ability was still intact when chasing home Klassical Dream, who had poached a 5l lead at the start, at Leopardstown on Boxing Day. However, with Klassical Dream, who disappointed after again pulling hard at Gowran in January, ridden more patiently at Cheltenham, the way was again open for Gavin Cromwell's 7yo to make the most of an uncontested lead. Danny Mullins judged the fractions to perfection and the combination stuck on strongly in the closing stages to beat Thyme Hill and the veteran Paisley Park. On the back of that win, the Liverpool Hurdle at Aintree looked his for the taking but, although he finished further in front of Thyme Hill and Champ than he had at Cheltenham, he had no answer to the late thrust of Sire du Berlais. His trainer said: 'Flooring Porter was a little bit fresh going to the start, and a little bit gassy during the race, but look, he ran a great race. It's disappointing to be beaten, but that's racing. He was beaten a length and a half – the best horse won, but he's still a very good horse and he'll probably aim for Cheltenham again next year.' The son of Yeats will be hard to stop next March, especially if he's allowed a similar amount of leeway in front.
GAVIN CROMWELL

GAELIC WARRIOR (GER) 4 b g

Everyone in racing seemed to want to be on Gaelic Warrior in the Boodles Juvenile Handicap Hurdle at the

Cheltenham Festival on the back of three encouraging runs in France in 2021. The switch to Willie Mullins coupled with the switch to handicaps made the market support all the more understandable and he ran a blinder on that first run for the yard despite being just touched off by the more experienced Brazil, who went on to finish third in Grade 1 company at Aintree on his next outing. Although the winner was impeded early and was carried slightly right on the approach to the home straight, the result might have been slightly different had Gaelic Warrior not persistently jumped out to his right. It was still a highly encouraging effort, however, and one that looked likely to set him up nicely for something at the right-handed Punchestown. However, that meeting came and went without his participation, but the 4yo son of Maxios figures on a handy mark and appeals strongly as just the type to win a decent handicap at around 2m this season. In fact, judged on his Flat-oriented pedigree, it'll be no surprise to see him in that sphere at some point in the not-too-distant future. WILLIE MULLINS

GALOPIN DES CHAMPS (FR) 6 bl g

Galopin des Champs has to go down as one of the unluckiest losers in recent Cheltenham Festival history. In a race that had cut up badly, this Grade 1 winner over both hurdles and fences had already taken the measure of main danger Bob Olinger a long way out in The Turners Novices' Chase and he was still on the bridle, some 12l ahead, when knuckling on landing and falling at the final fence with the race at his mercy. Fortunately, he got up unscathed and he confirmed his well-being by beating three inferior rivals in a Grade 1 at Punchestown a month later. He's a most interesting horse as he's won from 2m–3m over hurdles, but his four outings over fences have been around 2m4f–2m5f.

The 6yo could go either up or down in trip – probably with ease – and he possesses so much physical substance that it's hard to think his achievements so far are going to be the limit of his ability. After Punchestown, trainer Willie Mullins stated: 'I reckon Galopin Des Champs is a Gold Cup horse. I have to discuss that with Greg and Audrey [Turley, owners] but he looks a horse for the Gold Cup. He had a hard race at Cheltenham. Any horse that goes at that pace would have a hard race. All his homework suggested he was fine and Paul was happy with him. I was going to wait and go over three miles at Punchestown but then I thought about a Grade 1 race over two and a half miles here and we took our chance today. Paul rode him differently down to the first than he did at Cheltenham and that made a big change. To me it looked an ordinary pace and it looked like the other two elected to challenge him over the last three fences. Once he changed gear between the last two it was over bar jumping the last. He just seemed to be on a wrong stride and Paul let the horse decide. He put down lovely and got over it. He quickened away after the last and he couldn't pull him up going around the bend.' As with the likes of Facile Vega and Constitution Hill, his 2022-23 campaign is eagerly awaited and he could join the immortals if he turns out to be as good over 3m2f as he clearly is over shorter. WILLIE MULLINS

GALVIN (IRE) 8 b g

Until his last two runs in the Gold Cups at Cheltenham and Punchestown, Galvin's career had been one of steady improvement. Gordon Elliott's dual bumper winner won three of his five starts over hurdles but, as expected, really came into his own after being switched to chasing. It's a bit surprising that it took him five attempts to get off the mark over fences, but he has a fine strike-rate since that first chase win in July

2020 and he turned in his best effort in this sphere when landing last season's Grade 1 Savills Chase at Leopardstown in late December. That day he showed a tremendous attitude in the closing stages to beat the subsequent Cheltenham Gold Cup winner A Plus Tard by a short head, with the previous year's Paddy Power Gold Cup winner Kemboy back in third. The extra two furlongs of the Gold Cup (Cheltenham) looked sure to suit ideally but, although he wasn't far off his best, A Plus Tard stepped up considerably on the Savills form to reverse placings and to win in impressive fashion. Galvin's last run at Punchestown is best ignored as he was never really travelling with any fluency and was beaten a long way behind the impressive Allaho in the Punchestown Gold Cup over 3m. A summer off should have done him plenty of good and it's easy to forget that he's only an 8yo given all the racing he's had. Whether the plan this year is to go down the National route or to stick with the graded chases isn't public knowledge yet but, however his season unravels, he appeals strongly as the sort to win more races.
GORDON ELLIOTT

GELINO BELLO (FR) 6 b g

Steadily progressive in six runs over hurdles in the 2021-22 season, Gelino Bello should continue to improve as he embarks on his novice chasing career this term and Paul Nicholls is already licking his lips at that prospect: 'He's already jumped fences so bring on October. He's an exciting prospect and he can only get better.' His hurdles career yielded three wins, including a Grade 1 at Aintree in April, two second places, both behind Blazing Khal at Cheltenham, and a more than respectable fourth place in the Lanzarote Hurdle at Kempton in January, in which he was having just his sixth career start behind some battle-hardened rivals.

His Grade 1 win came in the Sefton Novices' Hurdle over 3m 149y and one would expect him to tackle that sort of trip as he goes over fences in the autumn. He's just 16-1 for the Brown Advisory Novices' Chase at the time of writing, but, given Paul Nicholls's dearth of runners at this year's festival, he may be a better prospect for the Mildmay Novices' Chase at Aintree a month later. Whatever his big-race targets, he will surely take a high rank in the novice chasing division as the season progresses. PAUL NICHOLLS

GERICAULT ROQUE (FR) 6 b g

Although Gericault Roque has yet to win over fences, he stepped up considerably on the form he'd shown over hurdles in a succession of tough-looking handicaps and he's the type to win a decent pot in the coming season. A hurdle scorer at Plumpton and Sandown in early 2021, he quickly showed he was at least as good over fences when third on his debut in this sphere at Wetherby in October over an inadequate 2m4f. However, the step up to 3m and beyond brought about further improvement and he deserves credit for his second placings over 3m5f at Warwick in January and on his final outing of the season in the Ultima Handicap at the Cheltenham Festival in March from out of the handicap. He's the sort to win either over hurdles or fences granted a sufficient test but, in the longer term, he looks just the sort to make up into a Grand National contender. Given his age and the fact that he's not been over raced, there's almost certainly more to come from him and a race like the Ladbrokes Trophy at Newbury in late November could be a good starting point. So far, he's raced on nothing quicker than good to soft but he seems to handle everything else. DAVID PIPE

GET IT RIGHT (IRE) 4 b g

Get It Right has bags of stamina in his pedigree – he's the first foal of a point winner, herself a half-sister to a point/2m4f chase winner – so it was highly encouraging to see him run so well over 2m in a Punchestown bumper on his debut in April. Despite his 25-1 starting price, he stuck on well in the last half mile (raced wide into the home turn) to finish fourth on good-to-yielding ground behind a Willie Mullins-trained winner, who was followed home by another from that stable and one from the Gordon Elliott yard. He's sure to come on a fair bit for that experience but, while he'll likely remain vulnerable in this type of event, he'll be of much more interest once he goes over hurdles and up in distance. Although only a 4yo, his future probably lies over fences but he'll also be of interest over hurdles granted a sufficient stamina test. He switched to Sean Aherne's yard in June having run for Desmond Kenneally for his debut run. SEAN AHERNE

GIN COCO (FR) 6 b g

Since being picked up for 80,000 euros following an encouraging hurdle debut at Pau in France on debut in May 2020, Gino Coco has only managed one start for Charlie Mann and two runs for Harry Fry. However, those last two runs came in the final two months of the season so he's hopefully over whatever kept him off the track for nearly a year and a half. The 6yo was backed into favouritism on his first outing for Fry at Fontwell in March and he didn't disappoint after his 500-day lay off, tanking through the race and easily winning by a wide margin on good ground. On the back of that he started favourite for a Punchestown event (2m, good to yielding) on his handicap debut in April and, although he was unable to follow up, he showed improved form to finish a close second of 25 behind Broomfield Hall in a race that has since thrown up Flat, hurdle and even chase winners. His pedigree suggests that he should stay 2m4f and there's certainly more improvement to come. He starts the season on an official BHA rating of 131 and it will be a surprise if he doesn't pick up a nice handicap assuming all remains well. HARRY FRY

GITCHE GUMEE 4 b g

A £65,000 purchase out of a sister to the very useful 2m4f/3m hurdle/chase winner Chilli Filli, Gitche Gumee made a fine start to his career in a 2m Kempton bumper in March which suggests he could be smart. He was under a ride turning in but he soon picked up the bridle and defied obvious greenness to score with plenty in hand from Kaleb and Diamond Egg, who were both having their second starts. The latter would frank the form next time by winning a Huntingdon bumper by nearly 4l and a few of the other beaten horses went to run well subsequently so the form looks okay. He was gelded at the end of that month so we didn't see him again, but his hurdles debut is awaited with interest and he could be very good. ALAN KING

GOWEL ROAD (IRE) 6 bb g

Gowel Road will be a useful addition to the chasing ranks this season and he's one to note between 2m and 2m6f, especially when there is plenty of give in the ground. The Nigel Twiston-Davies trained 6yo was an improved performer over hurdles last season and, although he only won once at Cheltenham (2m5f, good) in November, he posted his best efforts in Listed handicap company at Newbury later that month and in heavy ground after a break of nearly two months at Lingfield (heavy) in January. He was only seen out once after that effort but he dropped away in the closing stages to finish seventh (beaten just over 20l, a mistake at the fourth-last not helping matters) in the competitive Coral Cup, a race in which he started second favourite. His trainer does well with this type and, although he'll likely get a low-key introduction to fences, he's more than capable of making his mark in that new discipline. NIGEL TWISTON-DAVIES

HERMES DU GOUET (FR) 5 b g

Although he was a beaten favourite twice in bumpers last season, this winning pointer did enough to suggest in those two runs that he has a bright future as a jumper. He made his debut over 15.5f at Haydock in late December, where he finished second behind Forpaddytheplumber, with a yawning 11l back to the third horse. He was well backed beforehand which suggests that he had shown a bit at home, and, to his credit, he did show a willing attitude despite not quite being able to peg back the winner, who made most of the running. He had to settle for second again at Exeter six weeks later, this time behind Copper Cove over 2m 161y, a race in which he got outpaced by the winner from about 3f out before staying on again in the closing stages to close the gap to just over 2l at the line. He shaped as a stayer on both of those starts and he can soon get off the mark as a novice hurdler over slightly longer trips. Soft or heavy ground looks to suit him ideally and he may also need a stiff track to show his best. He looks the type of horse that his trainer excels with when the mud starts flying in the winter months and he has a bright future. VENETIA WILLIAMS

HIGHLAND CHARGE (IRE) 7 b g

A full brother to Do Your Job, who won three chases
for Michael Scudamore last season, including a
Grade 2 novice chase at Ayr in April, Highland Charge
progressed in all of his five starts over hurdles last
term, scoring twice at Naas over just shy of 2m
in February and March. The second of those wins
was a Grade 3 contest in which he touched off Vina
Ardanza, who ran well behind Jonbon in the Grade 1
Top Novices' Hurdle at Aintree on his next outing. A
lovely big horse, Highland Charge's trainer has always
regarded him as a chaser in the making, so it was
pleasing to see him achieve so much over hurdles. Do
Your Job is best at around 2m4f but this fellow may be
kept to shorter trips to start with before stepping up.
Soft ground suits him ideally so he should be able to
make hay over the winter. He has a very bright future.
NOEL MEADE

HILLCREST (IRE) 7 br g

Such was Hillcrest's rate of improvement throughout
the season that he started 9-4 favourite for the Albert
Bartlett at the Cheltenham Festival in March. He
never jumped or travelled with any conviction that
day, eventually pulling up before the race really started
in earnest. But wind the clock back to autumn. His
season started with a fluent win over 2m4f at Aintree
on his hurdle debut, staying on strongly in the closing
stages to beat Dan Skelton's Our Jet in a race that
threw up several winners. He followed up at Wetherby
(a straightforward task) but showed much-improved
form to win a Listed event at Cheltenham on New Year's
Day, a race that also worked out well. He was unlucky
to lose his rider early on back at that venue at the end
of January, but he made amends in style in very testing
ground at Haydock (Grade 2) when upped to 3m for

the first time, helping to force a decent gallop and powering clear in the straight to beat Crystal Glory (also included in the 100) by 8l. He may not have got over those exertions in the Albert Bartlett but nothing was found to be amiss at Cheltenham and, although he's the type to win again over hurdles, his future really lies over fences. He has a physique to back up his form – he's a huge, old-fashioned chasing type with chase blood in his pedigree (not surprising for one owned by the late Trevor Hemmings) – and it's not difficult to envisage him developing into a leading contender for the Brown Advisory Novices' Chase, especially if there is plenty of give in the ground. HENRY DALY

HULLNBACK 5 b g

Judging by Hullnback's pedigree, it's reasonable to assume that he's going to need a good test of stamina when he goes over hurdles. The 5yo is a half-brother to three point winners (one of whom won up to 3m over hurdles) out of a dam who won over 3m1f over hurdles. However, 2m on a soft surface proved enough of a test for him on his debut in a Chepstow bumper in November where he kept on strongly in the closing stages to win by just over 4l. He wasn't seen again for just over three months but, although he lost his unbeaten record, he stepped up on that debut form when finishing a respectable fifth to Top Dog in a Listed event at Newbury in February, making up plenty of ground in the straight to be nearest at the finish. The gelding sported a tongue-tie for his toughest assignment – a Grade 2 bumper at Aintree – and he turned in his best effort, finishing second of 18 behind Lookaway despite his rider becoming briefly unbalanced in the closing stages. He deserves plenty of credit for finishing as close as he did on that sharp track on goodish ground and he'll likely be able to build on that platform as he goes over 2m4f and beyond over hurdles this season. Fergal O'Brien, his trainer, has really come into his own in the last couple of seasons and Hullnback is worth keeping a very close eye on in the coming months. FERGAL O'BRIEN

IL ETAIT TEMPS (FR) 4 gr g

France has been a fantastic sourcing ground for Willie Mullins for a number of years and, although Il Etait Temps has yet to win a race, he showed more than enough in three hurdle starts at the highest level last season to think that he'll be able to rectify matters this time round. He was picked up after showing ability in a couple of French bumpers for Emmanuel Clayeux in spring of last year, but he must have been showing plenty at home as he was pitched straight into Grade 1 company for his hurdling debut and his first run for Mullins. He ran a fine race behind stable companion Vauban and Gordon Elliott's The Tide Turns at the Dublin Festival in early February and, while a bit further behind the same winner in the Triumph at Cheltenham, he shaped a bit better than the bare form given that he refused to settle. Although soundly beaten (again behind Vauban) at Punchestown, he may still have been feeling the effects of that Cheltenham race and his jumping was a little sticky at times. There'll be a host of opportunities for him – probably at a slightly lower level – in which he can gain a bit of confidence before going back to contest top-level races. He's only a 4yo so his best days are most certainly ahead of him and, judged on his pedigree, he should stay at least 2m4f. WILLIE MULLINS

JETARA (IRE) 4 b f

This filly is the first foal out of a bumper-winning sister to Jessica Harrington's Champion Hurdle winner

Jezki and she looked a smart prospect when winning a 2m4f Fairyhouse bumper in mid-April, in which she was taking on several rivals with previous experience. She beat the right horses too, having been delivered with a well-timed run by Michael O'Sullivan, who provides excellent value for his 7lb claim. The next two home were the Willie Mullins-trained pair Walk In The Brise and Cnoc Na Si, who both brought a decent level of form into the race. Jetara was pitched into the Grade 3 mares' bumper at the Punchestown Festival just 11 days later, with Jamie Codd booked for the ride, but she raced much too freely in the early stages in a slowly run race, ultimately dropping away from about 2f out to finish ninth, beaten 9½l by the winner The Model Kingdom. It was a big ask for one so inexperienced and the race may have come too soon as well, so she can easily be forgiven that effort. She ran a much better race in a bumper at the end of August, finishing third of 11 at Down Royal under Michael O'Sullivan in an above-average contest for the time of year, and she's now likely to be switched to hurdles. She's one to look forward to in that division for sure.
JESSICA HARRINGTON

JONBON (FR) 6 b g

As a brother to top-class 2m–2m4f hurdle and chase winner Douvan, Nicky Henderson's Jonbon has always come with much expectation. And, with the exception of his Supreme Novices' Hurdle run at Cheltenham where he – and the rest of the field – were taken apart by stable companion Constitution Hill, he has delivered every time he has set foot on a racecourse. His price soared to 570,000 euros after his debut point win in November 2020 and he landed the odds on his first run for the yard in a Newbury bumper in March of last year. He also created a good impression in winning his first three starts over hurdles last season at Newbury, Ascot and Haydock before coming unstuck at Cheltenham. However, he wasn't done for the season and a trip to Liverpool yielded a first success at the highest level when he stuck on determinedly to beat El Fabiolo, who might have prevailed but for meeting a bit of trouble and fluffing the last hurdle. Following the Aintree win, Henderson said: 'Jonbon has had a good campaign. He's a lovely, big, young horse and his future probably lies over fences. You have to admire him for the way he battled there, that was tough. He had to be brave and he was, very much so. Constitution Hill was the only horse to lower his colours but you can't take that out on him, he's unbeaten otherwise. He's finished up getting his Grade 1 here. I'm pretty certain he'll go over fences next season and he'll get further, I'm sure.' The 6yo has the physique to make up into a top chaser and he's one of the budding stars in what promises to be an enthralling season. NICKY HENDERSON

KATEIRA 5 b m

Dan Skelton is now firmly entrenched in the upper echelons of the training ranks and he's just as adept at training bumper winners as he is training hurdle or chase winners over the whole range of distances. Kateira is all about potential at the moment and, after winning nicely on her racecourse debut at Huntingdon in February, she was stepped up markedly in class for her next start in a Grade 2 bumper at the Grand National meeting at Aintree in April. In a race dominated by those ridden more forwardly, she made up a fair bit of ground in the closing stages to take fifth place, nearest at the finish. This half-sister to jump winners El Presente (2m3f–3m1f hurdle/smart chase) and Blairs Cove (2m–2m5f hurdle/chase) should be suited by

further than 2m judged on that Aintree run and, given her age and the fact that she's only had two outings, she's open to a considerable amount of improvement.
DAN SKELTON

KILLER KANE (IRE) 7 b g

A £300,000 purchase after winning an Irish point in March 2020, Killer Kane made a decent start to his chasing career last season, with six runs yielding two wins and three places. Having acquitted himself well in some good novice races in late 2021 and early 2022, he had his sights lowered slightly at Kempton in February and, wearing a first-time tongue-tie, he ran out a cosy winner of a 3m novices' handicap chase from the Nicky Henderson-trained Valsheda, who went on to frank the form next time out by winning a similar race at Ffos Las. Killer Kane was then stepped back up in grade but he proved up to the job, winning a 2m4f Listed novices' handicap chase at Sandown from Flic Ou Voyou with Dorking Lad, the winner of his previous two starts, back in third. He was then asked to contest a Grade 3 handicap chase over 3m 210y at Aintree and he ran another highly creditable race, finishing third of the 14 runners, albeit no match for Sam Brown and Shan Blue who filled the first two positions. It's possible that the extra yardage found him out so we can perhaps expect to see him back at around 2m4f when he returns to action. The handicapper has dropped him 1lb to a mark of 130 and that is certainly one he can still exploit. COLIN TIZZARD

KNAPPERS HILL (IRE) 6 b g

Knappers Hill did this publication proud last season, winning four races in seven starts, including one of the final races of the jumps season in late April at Sandown. His three defeats last term are all easily explained too

– firstly he ran a perfectly good race against Jonbon at Ascot in December, where he was beaten by just 5½l; he then ran a creditable race when sixth in the Betfair Hurdle in February at a time when the Nicholls' stable was under a bit of a cloud. Finally, he appeared not to handle the soft ground and possibly the 2m4f distance when down the field in a Grade 3 handicap hurdle at Sandown in March. His final two starts, a 2m1f novice hurdle at Newton Abbot in mid-April and a Class 2 handicap over 2m at Sandown a week later, showed him in a much better light and presumably he will be kept to shorter trips and better ground from now on. His early-season target is reportedly the Listed Gerry Feilden Hurdle at Newbury in late November and he may then embark on a chasing career at some point in the new year. He looks a smart prospect for fences for sure, but presumably Nicholls thinks that his current handicap mark of 141 as a hurdler is still workable. Whatever path is chosen for him, one thing is for sure – there are plenty more races to be won with him. PAUL NICHOLLS

LAW ELLA (IRE) 5 b m

A couple of hours after Gavin Cromwell had won his second Stayers' Hurdle with Flooring Porter, he had another winner with this mare, who ran away with a 2m1f Down Royal bumper despite taking on horses with previous racecourse experience. She's from the same family as Swamp Fox, who was rated 90 on the Flat and who also won over hurdles over 2m4f for Joe Murphy. Law Ella ran another fine race just three weeks later in the Grade 2 Mares' Bumper, again over 2m1f, at Aintree in early April, where she finished second to the Willie Mullins-trained Ashroe Diamond, who was running in her fourth bumper, having already won a race in May 2021. She saw it out well and, as often is the case with the Aintree race, the form has already started working out with Malina Jamila and Naughtinesse, who finished well behind the Cromwell mare, already winning over hurdles, and Magical Maggie, who was beaten a long way in tenth, winning a bumper at Bangor next time. Law Ella has the makings of a useful hurdler on those two runs with more improvement also likely as she starts moving up in distance. GAVIN CROMWELL

LEAVE OF ABSENCE (FR) 5 ch g

In the last five seasons Chris Gordon has had over 125 winners from over 850 runners at a strike-rate of around 14 per cent. His runners have earned in excess of £1.2m in win and place prize money. He had 26 individual winners last season, one of them being Leave Of Absence, who won his first two starts in bumper company. This half-brother to a couple of hurdle winners in France started second favourite for his racecourse debut at Kempton and justified the market support, beating one that had run well at Doncaster previously by 7l. He didn't really have to improve much to follow up at Newbury in a fairly uncompetitive event for the track, but he turned in his best effort in a Grade 2 bumper at Aintree on his final start, sticking on stoutly in the closing stages and finishing just behind Lookaway and Hullnback, who also get an entry in these pages. The 5yo is just the type to do well when sent over obstacles and, although he's unlikely to be pitched in at the deep end too early in his career, he should be able to pick up a couple of minor hurdle races before going up in grade. CHRIS GORDON

LOOKAWAY (IRE) 5 ch g

This 3m Irish point winner in November 2021 was bought for £170,000 before winning two bumpers for Neil King in the spring and he's a smashing hurdling prospect for that trainer this coming season. Fitted with a hood on his Rules debut over 2m at Newbury in February, he showed a professional attitude to grind out a workmanlike win from Fame And Concrete, a previous winner who was having his third start. He'd been well backed into 5-2 for that initial run and his trainer said afterwards: 'I'd hardly touched him, but when I gave him a gallop a week ago he wowed me.' He was sent off a fairly unconsidered 28-1 shot for the Grade 2 Aintree Bumper on his next start in April, but he confirmed himself a smart type by clearing away from a field chock-full of previous winners, with the result never really in doubt from a long way out. King reckons he's the best horse he's trained and that's saying something when you consider that he also handled Lil Rockerfeller, who won multiple races for him, including two Grade 2s, and who achieved an official rating of 160 at his peak. King said after Lookaway's Aintree win: 'I knew he'd come on a bundle, but when you come to Aintree for a race like this you don't know what you are taking on. There were a lot of nice horses from big stables who have won their races, and we are a small stable, but he's going to be a serious horse. I'm sure he'll go straight over hurdles next season and he'll start at two miles, although he'll stay further. He's already won a point, in which he jumped great. He jumps for fun, and I think he's everything, I really do. He's a point winner but he has speed. He's a lovely size too.' NEIL KING

L'HOMME PRESSE (FR) 7 b g

L'Homme Presse was one of the British success stories of last season, improving out of all recognition when sent over fences, his attacking, sound jumping style a feature of his five victories. With the benefit of hindsight, he was the proverbial 'good thing' running off 128 on his first chase start at Exeter (2m3f) in November and he thrashed subsequent winner Gunsight Ridge by 6l, with the pair pulling clear of the remainder. A graduation chase win at Ascot (2m5f) quickly followed before he made the transition into graded company. He impressed with the way he disposed of The Glancing Queen in the Dipper Novices' Chase at Cheltenham on New Year's Day but took his form to a higher level in a Grade 1 at Sandown (2m4f), jumping superbly in the lead and pulling well clear of subsequent Kim Muir runner up Mister Coffey in the closing stages. After that impressive win he looked a good thing for the Turners Novices' Chase at the Cheltenham Festival, but the decision was made to run him in the longer Brown Advisory (3m) instead. He upped his game even further there, again jumping soundly and showing a tremendous attitude to beat Ahoy Senor (also included in the 100) by 3½l. Trainer Venetia Williams said: 'L'Homme Presse has been absolutely fantastic. To be honest we have been thinking this is the most likely race from early days. The only way we would have gone shorter is if we got proper heavy ground but that was so unlikely. This rain has made it soft ground but not tiring ground. What a fabulous ride Charlie gave him, he did everything right. He took up the running when he needed to. We can dream about anything now.' His last run at Aintree, where he suffered his first defeat over fences, is best overlooked given he had probably had enough for the season and he failed by a long chalk to confirm placings with Ahoy Senor at a track that should have suited his running style. A summer break should have done him plenty of good and he appeals strongly as the type to win again at the highest level – a race like the King George at Kempton on Boxing Day (the ground is rarely overly testing at that venue) looks tailor-made for him. VENETIA WILLIAMS

MAHLER MISSION (IRE) 6 b g

John McConnell, who is based in County Meath in rural Ireland, has a decent strike-rate with his runners in the UK and all of Mahler Mission's four runs in 2022, three of which produced wins, were all on this side of the Irish Sea. Having caught the eye in two maiden hurdles in his native Ireland in the second half of 2021, he became McConnell's second-ever runner at Sedgefield in January as he scooted 14l clear of seven rivals in a 2m4f maiden hurdle, with the next three home all winning subsequently to give the form a solid look. He was upped in grade at Doncaster later the same month but he made light of it as he saw off six rivals in the Grade 2 River Don Novices' Hurdle, with five last-time-out winners unable to live with him. His trainer said: 'Mahler Mission is improving all the time, he isn't six until June and he's still a baby. I stuck him in the Albert Bartlett this week and he's definitely good enough to run, he won't disgrace himself.' The trainer was spot-on in that assessment as Mahler Mission ran an excellent race to finish seventh in a strong-looking renewal of that Grade 1 over 3m, which was won by The Nice Guy. His sights were lowered a bit at Perth the following month but he proved up to the task as he won a Listed novices' hurdle over 3m at the Scottish track, with horses trained by Paul Nicholls, Dan Skelton and Gordon Elliott filling the next three positions. He now has an official rating of 141 so he may be kept over hurdles in the short term to contest handicaps but, judged on his physique, the switch to fences will likely bring about further improvement and he looks an exciting prospect for the season ahead.
JOHN MCCONNELL

MAJOR DUNDEE (IRE) 7 b g

Everything about Major Dundee's pedigree suggested he'd be an improved performer when he tackled fences and he proved that with four good performances last season. This half-brother to point/hurdle/smart chase winner Onenightinvienna and prolific point winner Oh Toodles is out of a point winner, herself a granddaughter of a Thyestes Chase winner. So, not surprisingly, the 7yo bettered the pick of his hurdle form on his chase debut (handicap, 2m5f, good ground) at Fakenham in November, keeping on well to win a race in which three of the other four runners won next time out. He followed up at Bangor (soft) when upped to 3m the following month and, although he lost his unbeaten record over fences, he showed improved form when second behind Fuji Flight at Newbury in early March. His final start of the season came in the Scottish National and he ran respectably, finishing third behind two Christian Williams-trained runners, both of whom went on to run well in the bet365 Gold Cup at Sandown on the final day of the jumps season. A mark of 132 looks a good starting point for the new season and, assuming everything goes to plan, he should give a good account in some of the top staying chases. He's the type to strengthen up further this time round and, given that he seems to handle most ground, the Coral Welsh National could be a decent mid-season target. ALAN KING

MARBLE SANDS (FR) 6 gr g

Although form figures of 2022 in four hurdle starts doesn't make him look like a winning machine, there's plenty of substance to the form and this 6yo grey still has a progressive profile which suggests that he should soon be winning races. He made a promising start to his hurdling career at Lingfield in November, finishing 1l behind subsequent dual winner Milan Bridge, but he may well have beaten that rival had he not hit the last flight, causing him to lose momentum. He again put in some novicey jumps when finishing third of four behind Mr Glass at Newcastle over 2m6f later the same month, but they finished in a bit of a heap and Marble Sands would have preferred a stronger gallop. He then looked like getting off the mark at Taunton over 2m3f in January but he again hit the last, leaving the door open for Kingofthewest, who beat him by a neck. That rival went on to win again two starts later and they finished 6l clear of the third. Marble Sands' final run of the season at Sandown over 2m4f in March was by far his best run according to the ratings as he finished second of 17 in a Grade 3 handicap hurdle behind Complete Unknown. Again, a crucial mistake at the second-last flight probably cost him his chance victory but the form looks strong in any case with three of the horses in behind winning next time and the winner also running well in a Listed race next time out. There's clearly a pattern emerging in terms of his jumping letting him down at crucial stages, but if he can brush up on his technique he will surely win races. He's rated 123 which looks a fair starting point for the season ahead. FERGAL O'BRIEN

MASTER MCSHEE 8 b g

A quick glance at the form figures Master McShee achieved over fences last season may not look that inspiring with 31222 perhaps making it seem that he doesn't have a winning mentality. That is extremely harsh, however, as when you delve deeper into those runs you will see that he tended to come up against the very best Irish chasers throughout his novice season. On his chase debut in November he finished third behind Bob Olinger and Bacardys in an 18-runner beginners' chase and Master McShee quickly proved that run to have been no fluke by getting the better of Farouk D'Alene in a titanic tussle for the Grade 1 Faugheen Novice Chase at Limerick on

St Stephen's Day. Gabynako, who is no mug, was almost 30l behind that pair in third. He again contested a Grade 1 at the Dublin Racing Festival in February and, while he was no match for Galopin Des Champs, he was nicely clear of the remainder, which included the likes of Gaillard Du Mesnil and Fury Road. He then ran a cracker under a penalty in a Grade 2 over an inadequate 2m at Navan, where he was just unable to concede 7lb to Sizing Pottsie who beat him by ¾l. He again bumped into Galopin Des Champs at Fairyhouse on his final start of the season in April at Fairyhouse (2m4f) but he had Riviere D'Etel and Blue Sari behind him so he was anything but disgraced. It appears that trips of around 2m4f to 3m will be on the agenda now and, provided he stays away from Galopin Des Champs, he can surely win a few more Grade 1s in his second season. PADDY CORKERY

MERLIN GIANT (FR) 5 b g

Merlin Giant looks like one that should make his mark both on the Flat and over hurdles in the coming months. Emmet Mullins has been quietly making a name for himself in the last couple of years and his 5yo, who won a bumper at Ballinrobe last September, showed improved form to get off the mark on his second start over hurdles at the Galway Festival in July (2m). On the softest ground he's tackled so far and tried in a hood after his Flat run at the same course three days earlier, he travelled strongly before pulling clear in the closing stages to win with a bit in hand. Although he's Flat-bred he shaped that day as though he'd be worth another try over further (his debut over hurdles came over 2m3f). That form was boosted when third-placed Rexem (beaten 17l) won his next start and Merlin Giant appeals as the sort to do well in handicaps in that sphere. The 5yo has also shown ability on the Flat and will be one for handicaps in that discipline, too. EMMET MULLINS

MIGHTY POTTER (FR) 5 b g

Mighty Potter is another one of those that was soundly beaten behind potential superstar Constitution Hill in the Supreme Novices' Hurdle at Cheltenham in March. However, this half-brother to point/smart hurdle/chase winner French Dynamite and to 2m hurdle winner Indiana Jones, won three of his other four starts over hurdles, including one at Grade 1 level at Punchestown in April. Although his main rival Sir Gerhard, the odds-on favourite, underperformed in third spot that day, there was still plenty to like about the way he got the job done to beat Gatsby Grey, who ran to a similar rating as when successful at Naas on his previous outing. After that race, trainer Gordon Elliott stated he was a horse with a future, and that future is likely to include going over fences (probably sooner rather than later). The 5yo, who has only had six races so is open to plenty of improvement, is a strong-travelling sort who is essentially a fluent hurdler and he's sure to be well schooled ahead of his first outing over fences. GORDON ELLIOTT

MINELLA COCOONER (IRE) 6 b g

Willie Mullins has dominated the Cheltenham Festival for a few years now, but in 2022 he surpassed his best tally by racking up ten of the 28 winners over the four days, with five of them coming on the Friday. One horse who had to settle for second place on that stellar day was this former pointer, who filled that position in the Albert Bartlett Novices' Hurdle. The consolation for Mullins, however, was that he also trained the winner, The Nice Guy, who pulled 5l ahead of his stablemate after the last. That pair now head the market for this season's Brown Advisory Novices' Chase, but it is perhaps slightly surprising to see 12-1 still on offer for Minella Cocooner while The Nice Guy is just half those odds. Yes, there were 5l between the pair at Prestbury Park but it should be remembered that Minella Cocooner was sent off at 9-2 while The Nice Guy was an 18-1 poke and, when they met again at Punchestown six weeks later, the gap between them was just ¾l. Already a Grade 1 winner at the Dublin Racing Festival in February, Minella Cocooner is a year younger than The Nice Guy and he still has a bit of maturing to do as he demonstrated at Cheltenham by taking a keen hold. The pair may avoid each other until at least the Dublin Racing Festival, but it already promises to be a good tussle between them should they meet again over fences in the spring. Whether he can take the measure of The Nice Guy or not, Minella Cocooner looks well capable of adding to his trainer's Grade 1 tally and it would be no surprise to see him contesting the Gold Cups at Leopardstown and Cheltenham in the future. WILLIE MULLINS

MINELLA CROONER (IRE) 6 b g

Minella Crooner very much caught the eye when finishing second behind Minella Cocooner over 2m6f at the Dublin Racing Festival in February and the 6yo became the ante-post favourite for the Albert Bartlett on the back of that run before being ruled out due to a pulled muscle a week before the Cheltenham Festival. It was felt that Minella Cocooner had been given a clever ride from the front by Paul Townend at Leopardstown and that Minella Crooner, who finished just under 3l behind him, would be able to turn the tables over the slightly longer trip at Cheltenham, with the hill expected to suit this thorough stayer ideally. We will never know what would have happened but Minella Cocooner did finish runner-up in the Albert Bartlett behind The Nice Guy, which certainly gave the form a boost. Minella Crooner was a major disappointment at the Punchestown Festival, however, when he was pulled up in a race won by The Nice Guy, with Minella Cocooner ¾l behind him in second. That leaves him with a few questions to answer but Gordon Elliott has always thought of him as a staying chaser in the making and, based on his earlier efforts over hurdles last season, it is likely the Brown Advisory Novices' Chase will be the ideal race for him next season. He's currently a 25-1 shot for the race with Minella Cocooner available at just 12-1 and The Nice Guy at half those odds, so it can be argued that the value lies with the Elliott-trained horse, assuming that his Punchestown run was simply a blip. GORDON ELLIOTT

MONBEG PARK (IRE) 5 b g

Monbeg Park is bred to be a decent jumper – he's by Derby winner Walk In The Park out of an unraced sister to bumper/Flat/smart hurdle-high class chase winner Hidden Cyclone and to a 2m4f hurdle winner. He won his point and started at prohibitive odds for his debut in a bumper at Gowran in March but he was beaten a fair way by the easy winner Kalanisi Star. However, he stepped up on that performance to win an ordinary event at Cork (2m3f, soft to heavy) before continuing his run of steady improvement at Punchestown (back over 2m). That day he made up a fair bit of ground in the last half mile (despite his rider briefly losing an iron) but couldn't get near the more prominently ridden pair of Tag Man (Henry de Bromhead) and Sir Argus (Willie Mullins). Although the form of those bumpers is nothing out of the ordinary, he's the type to raise his game this season once he goes jumping and a step up to 2m4f should be to his liking. The 5yo is open to plenty of improvement and can win in either ordinary maiden or novice company before going into handicaps. SEAN THOMAS DOYLE

MY DROGO 7 b g

A smart unbeaten hurdler in 2020-21 who signed off with a Grade 1 win over 2m4f at Aintree in April, My Drogo's chasing bow in November was eagerly anticipated even though he faced just one rival, Gin On Lime, in a novice chase at Cheltenham. Everything was going perfectly for him as he jumped and travelled beautifully and he'd just taken up the running at the second-last and looked all over the winner when he knuckled on landing and slipped, leaving his sole rival to come home alone. There were still plenty of positives to be taken from the run, though, and one month later he made no mistake as he easily got the better of three rivals in a 2m4f 127y contest on the new course with runner-up Torn And Frayed franking the form in a competitive Grade 3 handicap in late January. He was as short as 7-1 for the Turners Novices' Chase at the Cheltenham Festival but two weeks later Dan Skelton announced that his star chaser, who was being prepared for the Dipper Novices' Chase on New Year's Day, was out for the rest of the season: 'We scanned him this morning after feeling heat in his near-fore tendon and whilst it is a very small lesion and will heal, it just requires time.' That was a blow but he can hopefully return this winter and perhaps the King George will no doubt be considered, assuming that he's lost none of his ability.
DAN SKELTON

NAME IN LIGHTS (IRE) 6 b g

A 90,000 euros purchase as a 3yo, this first foal of a maiden pointer made steady progress over hurdles last season and looks to have a bright future as he embarks on a novice chasing career. After placing three times in his first four starts over hurdles between November and early March, he came good at Wincanton at the end of March in decisive fashion, beating a couple of solid yardsticks, and that race has already started working out. Carrying a penalty for that win, he made light of it at Kempton three weeks later, winning comfortably from the Emma Lavelle-trained Rocky Lake. He's now rated 123 over hurdles and he may contest a handicap or two off that mark in the early part of the season, but it's assumed that he will go chasing sooner or later. Both his hurdles wins were achieved over 2m but he should stay a bit further. JOE TIZZARD

NORTH LODGE (IRE) 5 b g

This brother to a bumper winner and half-brother to winners in bumpers, over hurdles and over fences, only had four runs last season, but he ended the campaign as a progressive, Grade 1-placed gelding who is likely to step up on those achievements in the coming season. Alan King introduced the 68,000-euro purchase in a novices' hurdle in December and he overcame his inexperience in very gusty conditions to nail the two market leaders (both previous winners) in the closing stages. On that evidence the step up to 2m4f looked likely to suit and so it proved on his next outing at Cheltenham at the end of January, where he showed a good attitude to follow up in a Grade 2 novices' hurdle. Although he tasted defeat for the first time at Kelso in March (also a Grade 2), he only went down by a short head to Nells Son, a run that encouraged connections to take in the Grade 1 at Aintree (2m4f) the following month. He wasn't far off his best, keeping on in a manner that suggested he should stay a bit further this time round. King said: 'It was a lovely run and North Lodge is an exciting young horse. He stayed on well and I would think we'll stick to the handicap route with him from an experience point of view. He's only learning and we've just scratched the surface with him.' He's effective from 2m1f–2m4f (and is bred to stay a bit further judged on pedigree) and handles good and soft ground. He's only a 5yo so it'll be a disappointment if he doesn't add to his tally in the coming months. ALAN KING

NUCKY JOHNSON (IRE) 4 b g

Noel Meade is starting afresh this season having recently parted company with stable jockey Sean Flanagan, but there'll be no shortage of quality riders to fill the gap at a yard that tasted Grade 1 success with Beacon Edge in last season's Drinmore. Nucky Johnson has some way to go before he makes it to graded level, but he shaped encouragingly on his debut in a Punchestown bumper in April when third of 15 runners behind a Gordon Elliott-trained winner. Despite racing on the outside, he got within striking distance of the leaders inside the last half-mile, but he was unable to pick up in the closing stages. The 4yo is sure to come on a fair bit for that experience and, although it's not easy to predict what his best trip will be at this stage (he has Flat winners and a smart staying hurdle/chase winner in Brave Eagle in his pedigree), he'll probably stay at least 2m4f. It's not clear whether he'll take in another bumper or go straight over hurdles, but he's certainly capable of better and looks sure to win races. NOEL MEADE

NURSE SUSAN (FR) 5 ch m

A half-sister to two very useful Irish jumpers, including the ill-fated Le Martalin, Nurse Susan was impressive when winning a 2m1f maiden hurdle at Carlisle by 7½l in November, and her rider Harry Skelton admitted afterwards that she was held in very high regard at her yard: 'We thought a lot of Nurse Susan at home but you just never know going to the track for the first time. She's something a bit special, hopefully.

She's a proper National Hunt mare, who's only four, and whatever she does this year will be a bonus.' She comfortably got the better of Zabeel Champion, a winner of his previous start, in a 1m7f 113y contest at Leicester the following month, after which she was upped in grade as she contested a Class 2 mares' novices' hurdle at Lingfield, where she was outstayed by the very smart Love Envoi on her first start in heavy ground. The pair met again in the mares' novices' hurdle at the Cheltenham Festival and Harry Fry's mare was able to confirm the form, beating Nurse Susan by slightly further than she had at Lingfield. Nevertheless, in finishing fourth of 19 in that Grade 2 event, she ran a perfectly sound race, doing best of the 5yos. An official rating of 129 looks fair enough, given that she is open to further progress, and perhaps she will also improve for a step up in trip. DAN SKELTON

ODIN'S QUEST 4 b g

A half-brother to several winners (mainly on the Flat but also a couple over hurdles), out of Sablonne, who was a winner over 1m, Odin's Quest probably didn't beat much when winning a 2m bumper at Huntingdon in January, but he did it nicely, travelling all over his rivals and quickening clear of the odds-on favourite Propelled in the closing stages. The form has taken a few knocks since with that Nicky Henderson-trained runner-up beaten again in a bumper and a novice hurdle subsequently, but you can only beat what's in front of you and the manner of the victory did suggest that Odin's Quest has a touch of class. The fact that he was well backed for his debut would also imply that he is highly thought of and we shall find out more about him when he tackles hurdles this autumn. His tactical speed will certainly benefit him in such races and he can most definitely add to his tally. GARY MOORE

OUR POWER (IRE) 7 b g

Having lost his form for Nigel Twiston-Davies as a hurdler the previous season, Our Power found a new lease of life as a handicap chaser for Sam Thomas last term and his six runs in late 2021 and early 2022 yielded two wins plus a couple of excellent runs in two of the top handicap chases to be contested in February and March. He won two small-field handicaps over 2m4f at Wincanton in December and Huntingdon in January before acquitting himself well when stepped up to 3m in the Grade 3 Coral Trophy at Kempton in February, where he finished third behind the Christian Williams-trained pair of Cap Du Nord and Kitty's Light. He appeared to stay the trip well in Surrey but he perhaps didn't quite get home over 3m1f when he next ran in the Ultima Handicap Chase at Cheltenham. Nevertheless, he finished a highly creditable fifth behind Corach Rambler and he's since been dropped a couple of pounds by the handicapper, which seems generous. He looks an ideal type for races like the Paddy Power Gold Cup at Cheltenham in November or the *Racing Post* Gold Cup in December, both of which are run over around two and a half miles. He certainly looks capable of landing a big pot this term for his up-and-coming handler. SAM THOMAS

PARTY BUSINESS (IRE) 6 b g

Placed in three bumpers in early 2021, Party Business had a busy time of it as a novice hurdler last term, running seven times between November and May, winning twice. His first win came on his second start in mid-December, when he took the notable scalp of City Chief in a 2m5f 141y maiden hurdle at Ascot, with Complete Unknown, who would go on to win a Grade 3 hurdle later in the season, back in third. A faller in the Challow Hurdle two weeks later, where he might have finished second behind Stage Star if he'd stood up, he then ran a rare poor race at Warwick in mid-January, but perhaps the combination of his fall in the Challow and having three quick races in succession took their toll. He bounced back to form in the Martin Pipe Handicap Hurdle at Cheltenham, finishing fifth behind Banbridge after coming from a most unpromising position having been badly hampered by a faller early on. He got a trouble-free run on his next start, which was a Grade 3 handicap hurdle over 3m1f on Grand National day at Aintree, where he edged out Ilikedwayurthinking, with that pair well clear of the third. He then ran another good race when fourth of 16 behind Romeo Brown in another 3m handicap hurdle at Haydock in May, where, like at Aintree, he needed plenty of stoking. Now rated 141, that was probably his final run over hurdles with his trainer saying: 'We'll go chasing with him next season. He's bred to be a chaser so let's get on and do that.' IAN WILLIAMS

PATH D'OROUX (FR) 5 b g

The first foal of a French 2m1f hurdle winner, Path D'Oroux fetched £105,000 after winning a point on his second start and it looks like it was money well spent on the evidence of his first run in a 23-runner bumper over 2m at Punchestown in late April. He was quite keen early but, asked to go and win his race, he responded generously for pressure in the closing stages. His trainer Gavin Cromwell said afterwards: 'Path D'Oroux is a nice horse. I'm delighted with that as we really liked him at home and I'd say it was a good bumper. He was a little bit keen and it didn't exactly go to plan. We intended to ride him with a little bit of cover and, while we couldn't get it, he still won and that's always the sign of a good one.' He's one to look forward to over hurdles and the sky's the limit for him. GAVIN CROMWELL

PEKING ROSE 7 br g

Given his age, his connections, his pedigree and his form over hurdles, there's every reason to expect Peking Rose to raise his game once his attentions are switched to chasing. Fergal O'Brien's 7yo, who had already won a bumper and a soft-ground 'introductory' hurdle at Newbury, wasn't far off his best when upped to 2m4f back at the same venue in March, finishing second behind Gelino Bello, who would win a Grade 1 on his next start. On his final start of the season on his handicap debut at Aintree, Peking Rose didn't figure, but he was far from disgraced, finishing seventh of 21 in a Grade 3 won by Langer Danl. His trainer is on record saying that he's not been the easiest to keep right (he'd reportedly hurt his back in 2020) but he managed five runs last season and hopefully his problems are now a thing of the past. He's more a handicap project at present and his progress will be followed with interest. FERGAL O'BRIEN

POETIC MUSIC 4 ch f

Mofeyda, who is the dam of several Flat winners, has had four of her offspring try (unsuccessfully) to win a jumps race but Poetic Music appeals as the one that can redress that balance in the coming season. The 4yo showed steady improvement to win her first three starts in bumpers at Market Rasen, Newbury and Cheltenham (Listed) but her unbeaten record came to an end when she took on the 'big boys' in the Championship bumper at the Cheltenham Festival. Although no match for the likes of Facile Vega and American Mike, she deserves credit for her sixth placing, especially as she was the only filly and the only 4yo in the race. The way she saw out those bumper runs suggests she'll have no problems with the step up to around 2m4f and there's a decent programme of mares-only races should connections decide to go down that route in the short term. The daughter of Poet's Voice is open to plenty of improvement as a lightly raced sort and she handles both good and soft ground. FERGAL O'BRIEN

REDEMPTION DAY 5 b g

A £40,000 Goffs UK purchase as a 2yo out of an unraced sister to 2011 Champion Bumper winner Cheltenian, Redemption Day made the perfect start to his career at Leopardstown in late December as he eased clear of next-time-out winner Music Day in a 2m bumper at Leopardstown. He was put away for the Champion Bumper at Cheltenham following that impressive display but the heavy rain that arrived on the Wednesday at Cheltenham was completely against this speedy type and he trailed in a remote 13th of 15 finishers behind Facile Vega and American Mike. He took on that pair again in the Punchestown Champion Bumper six weeks later where he was able to show his true colours on the good-to-yielding ground, looming up menacingly under Jody Townend around 2f out before keeping on doggedly after being headed in the final furlong by Facile Vega, with just 1¼l separating them at the finish. Fourteen lengths behind them was American Mike so the form looks reliable. Mullins has a clear soft spot for Facile Vega, who is now the strong favourite for the Supreme Novices' Hurdle in ante-post lists, but he was perhaps surprised to see how close Redemption Day got to him at Punchestown. He said: 'I just knew that we'd got one good horse and Patrick [Mullins] keeps telling me that Redemption Day is a good horse too, so he's proved his point there. Facile Vega had to pull it out there because Jody nearly stole it. She said "we didn't beat him, but we frightened him".' WILLIE MULLINS

SAMARRIVE (FR) 5 b g

Still only a 5yo, Samarrive keeps his place in this list having won two races for us last season from just five starts. The first of those came in a Listed handicap hurdle over 2m at Sandown in early December where he kept on strongly to pull 8½l clear of Zambezi Fix and Thibault. Raised 11lb for that, he was then bitterly disappointing in a Grade 3 handicap over the same trip at Ascot two weeks later, losing touch from about four out before being pulled up. Given a break after that, he ran a better race in the Imperial Cup back at Sandown in mid-March, finishing ninth behind Suprise Package, but he still had a few questions to answer at that stage. However, he answered those questions loudly and clearly by winning his final start of the season, a 2m4f handicap at Sandown, which he won with more in hand than the 5l winning margin would suggest. The longer trip seemed to suit him well and it could be that he is kept to hurdles for now, although an official rating of 143 will make life harder for him. He could be the sort to make a really useful chaser and there are more races to be won with him in that sphere. PAUL NICHOLLS

SKYTASTIC (FR) 6 b g

Skytastic bombed out on his only attempt in Grade 1 company when finishing down the field in the Grade 1 Sefton Novices' Hurdle at Aintree in April, but he showed enough in a light campaign over hurdles last season to suggest he's very much one to keep on the right side in the coming months. The Sam Thomas-trained 6yo, who won his two bumpers in the 2020-21 season, made light of an 11-month absence to score on his hurdles debut back at Doncaster in January, form that was franked by the subsequent wins of the runner-up, third, fourth and sixth. He went to

Ascot on softer ground next time but showed a good attitude to keep his unbeaten record intact, holding on by a neck in a race over 2m3f that also threw up its share of winners. The lure of Graded racing proved too tempting to ignore but he didn't get home on his first run beyond an extended 2m3f when finishing a well-beaten tenth at Aintree over 3m 149y on his final start in April. That trip was probably too far for this Flat-bred at this stage and he'll be of interest back in trip from what looks a workable handicap mark this season. He's a fluent jumper with a decent cruising speed and it wouldn't surprise if he was able to drop back successfully to 2m this season. The Betfair Hurdle at Newbury in February or the Coral Cup at the Cheltenham Festival could turn out to be suitable targets and this scopey sort is open to plenty of improvement. SAM THOMAS

SOFT RISK (FR) 6 b g

Soft Risk's record so far is a healthy one – four wins from six starts in a bumper and over hurdles – with the definite promise of more to come. This £40,000 purchase as a 3yo made his debut in an Ayr bumper in May 2021 and he justified his position near the head of the market to win easily. Almost 200 days later he returned to the same course for his hurdles debut and he created a favourable impression in winning an ordinary event by 5l. Two wins at Kelso followed in winter (heavy and good-to-soft) but, ironically, he turned in his best efforts on his last two starts – when finishing second both times, the most recent when chasing home a well-handicapped sort in Platinumcard, who was having his first run for Gordon Elliott. That gives the Nicky Richards-trained 6yo a solid platform with which to start the new season and he's the type to take his form to a higher level. His current BHA rating of 128 looks workable and, given the yard is renowned for its exploits with chasers, it won't surprise to see him over fences at some point. However, handicap hurdles in the North are likely to be the way forward in the short term and he's sure to add to his tally. NICKY RICHARDS

SOLDIER OF DESTINY (IRE) 6 b g

Jamie Snowden had another good season in 2021-22 with 49 jumps winners at a 19 per cent strike-rate while a whopping 53 per cent of his runners finished in the top three, which is no mean feat. One horse who looks to have a very bright future is Soldier Of Destiny, a point winner who won two of his four chases at the start of this year. He won his second outing at Ffos Las in February, a novices' handicap chase over 2m3f which has worked out exceptionally well. He finished 8l in front of Longshanks, who went on to win his next start by 18l and there was a further 4l back to Yggdrasil, who won his next two outings. The fourth home, Pride Of Lecale, also went on to win a handicap chase two starts later. Soldier Of Destiny jumped superbly, and that was also the case on his next start at Newbury over 3m, although he sprawled on landing at the last and that cost him his chance as he ran out a gallant third behind Fuji Flight and Major Dundee. 3m also appeared to stretch his stamina to the limit so it was no surprise to see him drop back to 2m4f on his final start in late March at Haydock. There he beat Burrows Diamond, the winner of his previous two starts, with clear daylight back to his other three rivals, who would all go on to win their next races. Rider Gavin Sheehan said afterwards that Soldier Of Destiny would be given a break after that run and we didn't see him again last season, but there is still mileage in his handicap mark of 137 when he returns, given that he's an improving 6yo. JAMIE SNOWDEN

STATE MAN (FR) 5 ch g

One of Willie Mullins's five winners on the final day of the Cheltenham Festival this year was State Man, who was sent off at odds of 11-4 for the 26-runner County Hurdle even though it was just his fifth career start over hurdles. He justified those cramped odds in good style, however, coming through smoothly from about the second last to comfortably see off First Street, Colonel Mustard and West Cork. The trainer's reaction afterwards was telling: 'State Man could easily have gone to the Supreme Novices', and we'll go back Graded race hurdling probably after this. Perhaps we'll go for the top level at Punchestown.' He did indeed contest a Grade 1 in late April and he made light of it as he saw off four rivals, headed by dual Grade 2 scorer Flame Bearer, by an easy 7l in the Champion Novice Hurdle. That was over 2m3f but he certainly has the speed and class to go back to two miles and he appeals as a Champion Hurdle contender, assuming of course that Mullins is brave enough to take on both Honeysuckle and Constitution Hill. Should they decide to switch to fences immediately then odds of 14-1 for the Arkle at the time of writing certainly would look tempting. WILLIE MULLINS

STATTLER (IRE) 7 br g

At the time of writing it's not clear whether Stattler will be having a Gold Cup preparation or if he'll be going down the Grand National route. He's best priced 20-1 for the Gold Cup and around 25-1 for the Aintree spectacular, but it's a nice 'problem' for Willie Mullins to have at this stage. It really could go either way as he developed into a high-class and unbeaten novice chaser last season, with wins in a beginners' chase at Fairyhouse and a Grade 3 at Naas in January confirming he was already a better chaser than a hurdler. He reserved his best effort for the National Hunt Chase (3m5f) at the Cheltenham Festival, a race his owner Ronnie Bartlett had won in 2018 with Rathvinden and in 2021 with Galvin. That day, he travelled supremely well before pulling clear in the closing stages to beat market leader Run Wild Fred by 8l. That ended up being his final start of the season but this strapping 7yo, who is still open to a good deal of improvement, is capable of making the transition to Grade 1 company this time around, granted a suitable test of his stamina. He stays particularly well, he jumps soundly in the main and, although he has yet to tackle a sound surface, he seems to handle most other conditions. His participation is going to heighten interest in what already is shaping up to be a fantastic season. WILLIE MULLINS

STRINGTOYOURBOW (IRE) 5 ch g

Christian Williams is making a bit of a name for himself with his staying chasers and he's already landed the Welsh National with Potters Corner (who also won the lockdown virtual Grand National!) in 2019, as well as Win My Wings, who won this year's Eider and Scottish National, in the last-named race leading home a one-two for the yard with Kitty's Light finishing a gallant second. Stringtoyourbow has yet to race over fences but his dam is a half-sister to a 2m5f/3m hurdle and chase winner from the family of Grand National-winner Red Marauder so staying trips over fences are likely to prove his metier. After an inauspicious first three runs over hurdles, the step up to 3m brought about a big chunk of improvement and he barely came off the bridle to beat a competitive field comprising several previous winners at Ayr in early April. After that win his trainer said: 'Stringtoyourbow is a horse we like. He's been too keen in his maiden and novice hurdles but he's a nice horse going forward and I'll try to find something for him at Punchestown.' That meeting came and went without his participation but, although he was raised 14lb for his Ayr victory, a mark of 115 still leaves him looking leniently treated for the forthcoming season. It wouldn't surprise to see him over fences sooner rather than later and there's a chance he could go straight into handicaps in that sphere. The 5yo is a nice prospect. CHRISTIAN WILLIAMS

SUPER SIX 5 b g

A dual bumper winner who finished fifth behind Sir Gerhard in the 2021 Champion Bumper at Cheltenham, Super Six jumped indifferently on his hurdles bow at Perth in September but he showed a good attitude as he forced a dead-heat with It's Good To Laugh, who won again next time, with that pair pulling 12l clear of the remainder. He finished fifth on his next two starts at Ascot and Chepstow, racing very keenly both times, but he ran a better race on his handicap debut in mid-March at Taunton over 2m 104y, finishing second behind Dibble Decker, who brought some good form into the race. Super Six built on that performance next time at Market Rasen over 2m2f 140y, outpointing Doctor Ken, who was sent off the odds-on favourite, in a driving finish. He again showed a good attitude to get his head in front and that will stand him in good stead as he starts novice chasing. He will probably stay around 2m4f as a chaser but expect him to be kept away from quick ground as he seems to prefer a bit of cut. NIGEL TWISTON-DAVIES

TARAHUMARA 6 b g

A full brother to a bumper winner out of a chase/ hurdle winner for Robert and Sally Alner, Tarahumara ran twice over hurdles last season and he gave the impression that there is plenty more to come from him as his career progresses. He finished a clear second of 12 on his debut at Wincanton (soft) over 1m7f in early January, making steady headway from the rear after three out to finish 5l behind the more experienced Great Ocean with just over 6l back to the third. He improved on that on his next start over 2m at Chepstow in April, where he cruised through from about two out to win with more authority than the 7½l margin of victory suggests. It may not have been the strongest race of its type, with the favourite Hermes Boy underperforming, but it was still impressive the way that he galloped all over them. A big, scopey type by the sire of Edwardstone amongst others, he had clearly come on plenty from his debut in and he handled the quicker ground fine too. He is in good hands and should make a decent chaser in time, but there are more races over hurdles to be won with him first. EMMA LAVELLE

TEDDY BLUE (GER) 4 b g

The winner of a 1m6f maiden on the Flat for Francois-Henri Graffard at Saint-Cloud in September, Teddy Blue was sold privately in late January of this year and switched to Gary Moore by his new owners. It was probably just a fact-finding mission at Lingfield just two weeks later, but the 4yo performed well, finishing second to My Silver Lining in a 2m novices' hurdle after racing freely in the early stages. He readily moved to the front two out before those early exertions took their toll in the heavy ground but plenty of encouragement could be drawn from the run. He massively improved on that next time in the Grade 2 Adonis Juvenile Hurdle at Kempton, where he was about to lay down a serious challenge to Knight Salute when making a mess of the final obstacle and he ultimately had to settle for second behind that rival, who was completing a five-timer. He again raced freely so it was to his credit that he was still in there pitching at the business end. He was keen again in the Triumph Hurdle on his next start and, after not jumping fluently throughout, he was never able to land a blow, a first-time hood not appearing to help him settle. Hopefully he will learn to relax better in his races and, when he does, he will surely win races over hurdles as he clearly has a powerful engine. GARY MOORE

TELMESOMETHINGGIRL (IRE) 7 b m

One of Henry De Bromhead's six winners at the 2021 Cheltenham Festival was Telmesomethinggirl, who hosed up in a strong-looking edition of the Mares' Novices' Hurdle under Rachael Blackmore. Last season revolved around a tilt at the Grade 1 Mares' Hurdle on the opening day of Cheltenham and things had gone well for her in the build-up as she showed enough in her two runs on winter ground in late 2021 to suggest that she could be competitive, while the good-to-soft ground at Prestbury Park in March also promised to suit her ideally. It was all going perfectly for her during the race as well with the mare appearing to have plenty left in the tank as they approached the second-last. However, at that point the dream came to an abrupt end as she tripped over Indefatigable, who fell heavily just in front of her. It was too early to say how she would have fared, of course, but it seems very likely that she would have taken a hand in the finish. The good news was that she emerged relatively unscathed and she recovered in time to meet a few of the same rivals in the Grade 1 Mares' Champion Hurdle at the Punchestown Festival. However, that race ended early too as she took a fall four from home, again far too early to know what might have happened. Those were her first non-completions in 14 starts over hurdles and she's usually a slick jumper, so it's far too soon to give up on her. Still only seven, her season will surely be geared around another tilt at the Cheltenham race on day one of the festival and 12-1 on offer at the time of writing makes plenty of appeal, especially as a few in front of her in the betting are unlikely to make the race. It's also worth remembering that she was only 4-1 for the mares' race last March and it's not as if there are loads of alternative targets for her.

HENRY DE BROMHEAD

THE NICE GUY (IRE) 7 b g

Of the ten Willie Mullins-trained winners at the Cheltenham Festival in March, only one was returned at bigger than 11-4 and that solitary winner was The Nice Guy, who was an 18-1 shot in the Albert Bartlett Novices' Hurdle. The 7yo, who is out of a three-quarter sister to Grade 1 hurdle winner Massini's Maguire, was making just his fourth racecourse appearance, having only made his debut in a bumper at Fairyhouse in November. He'd only had his first outing over hurdles at the end of January at Naas over 2m3f, which he won by 8l, with the third, fourth and fifth all winning next time out. He was understandably still novicey at Cheltenham, but he showed plenty of class as he made steady headway before the second-last before drawing 5l clear from stablemate Minella Cocooner after the final flight with the rest of the field left trailing in their wake. The Nice Guy shows little at home, which may explain the big SP, but Mullins said after his victory: 'He just keeps improving all the time. Malcolm [Denmark, owner] got him as he wants a good chaser and, hopefully, he will make a nice novice chaser next year.' The Nice Guy backed up his Cheltenham win by also winning the Grade 1 Novices' Hurdle at the Punchestown Festival over 3m in April, again from Minella Cocooner, although this time there was only three quarters of a length to separate them. That victory underlined his status as the best staying novice hurdler around and he rightly heads the betting for the 2023 Brown Advisory Novices' Chase, with a switch to fences planned for the autumn. He is bound to eke out further improvement as he embarks on his chasing career and he is very much one to keep onside. WILLIE MULLINS

UNANSWERED PRAYERS (IRE) 6 b g

Having shown promise in bumpers after being placed in points, Unanswered Prayers had a productive first season over hurdles with three wins, three seconds and two fourths to show for his eight runs (he would have had four wins but for being somewhat harshly demoted from first place at Warwick in November for causing interference). His wins came in a fairly decent 2m maiden hurdle at Uttoxeter in October, a 2m5f novice hurdle at Wincanton in January in which he got the better of the useful Flemenstide and another novice hurdle race over 2m4f 114y at Plumpton in March, where he just managed to wear down the front-running Hecouldbetheone in the closing stages. Chris Gordon said after that last win: 'It was a really game performance from Unanswered Prayers and he's a gorgeous horse. I thought we were going to do it quite well from the second last but the other horse came back to him and it was a real scrap. I think there are two tough novices there. We might have one more run with him this season, we'll see what he looks like. I am looking forward to going chasing with him next season.' He did run once more, in a novices' handicap at Plumpton in April, where he finished a close second to Bourbali, who was completing a hat-trick, and he again showed a likeable attitude on ground that was almost certainly too quick for him. He should have another productive campaign over fences, perhaps staying at around 2m4f to start with but maybe stepping up to 3m eventually. It is also likely that he will be kept away from good ground as all his best runs so far have come with plenty of cut. CHRIS GORDON

WEST CORK WILDWAY (IRE) 8 br g

West Cork Wildway's overall form is a bit uneven but the 8yo knows how to win (he's won a bumper, two hurdles and a chase) and he's better than he was able to show on his final start at Killarney in May when turned out fairly quickly on the back of an encouraging run at Punchestown. Paul O'Flynn's chaser showed he was just as effective over fences as he was over hurdles when winning on his second run in this sphere at Thurles in November (2m6f, good) but, although he didn't better that form on three chase starts afterwards, he shaped well after a near four-month break at Punchestown in late April, his stamina just ebbing away in the closing stages on that first run over 3m. However, given he's by Yeats out of a Presenting mare, there's enough in his pedigree to suggest he will prove fully effective over 3m in due course and he's open to improvement after just five runs over fences. He handles most ground from good to heavy and there could be a decent mid-range handicap coming his way if he's able to raise his game again this time round. PAUL O'FLYNN

WESTERN ZARA (IRE) 6 gr m

Western Zara, who cost £85,000 and is the first foal of a half-sister to a 2m3f hurdle winner, is an unexposed sort from a good yard and is the type to win more races in the 2022-23 season. This dual hurdle winner at Clonmel (2m2f, soft) and Fairyhouse (2m7f, good to yielding) stepped up on the form she'd shown in that sphere when scoring back at Clonmel on his chasing debut (2m4f, heavy) in early March. She bettered that effort switched to handicap company at Punchestown on her handicap debut and her only subsequent start next time. Although she was no match for Anthony Honeyball's previous winner Lilith, she wasn't beaten far, leaving the impression that a return to 3m would be to her liking. Her jumping was sound in the main, she's a strong-travelling sort who, at the age of six, is just the sort to raise her game again this time round. Her current Irish mark of 130 gives her a bit of room for manoeuvre and the daughter of Westerner, who is out of a Flemensfirth mare, is the type to win more races – either against the boys or in mares-only races (all bar one of her races under Rules have so far been in the latter category). PAUL NOLAN

WINTER FOG (IRE) 8 b g

Although he wasn't at his very best on his last two starts at Aintree and on his reappearance at Kilbeggan, it's well worth giving Winter Fog another chance to confirm the promise of his form at Leopardstown in December and at the Cheltenham Festival in March. Both those runs came on soft ground and that may well be the key to his future prospects and he's taken to improve a record that so far reads one win from eight starts over hurdles. He showed much-improved form on his first run for the Emmet Mullins yard in a Pertemps qualifier on his handicap debut in December when he chased home Panda Boy, who has since won over fences (a race which also threw up other winners). But he reserved his best effort for the final of that series at Cheltenham, where he fared best of the Irish contingent behind Third Wind in fourth while sporting the hood for the first time. That is a solid piece of form and he's very much the type to win a competitive handicap around 3m. His dam is a sister to a 2m6f chase winner and, although he'll be 9yo at the turn of the year, he'd also be interesting if switched to fences at some point this season. EMMET MULLINS

INDEX

ADAMANTLY CHOSEN (IRE)	3
AHOY SENOR (IRE)	4
ALAPHILIPPE (IRE)	4
ALTOBELLI (IRE)	5
AMERICAN MIKE (IRE)	6
APPRECIATE IT (IRE)	6
ASHDALE BOB (IRE)	7
AUTUMN RETURN (IRE)	8
AUTHORISED SPEED (FR)	8
BALCO COASTAL (FR)	9
BALLYGRIFINCOTTAGE (IRE)	10
BARDENSTOWN LAD	11
BEAUPORT (IRE)	12
BLAZING KHAL (IRE)	12
BOOMBAWN (IRE)	13
BRIDGE NORTH (IRE)	14
BRING ON THE NIGHT	14
CALL OF THE WILD (IRE)	15
CATCH THE SWALLOWS (IRE)	16
CHAMPAGNE TOWN	16
CHANGING THE RULES (IRE)	17
CITY CHIEF (IRE)	17
COBBLERS DREAM (IRE)	18
CONSTITUTION HILL	19
CORACH RAMBLER (IRE)	20
CRYSTAL GLORY	21
DALAMOI (IRE)	21
DINOBLUE (FR)	22
DUBROVNIK HARRY (IRE)	23
DUSART (IRE)	23
EDITEUR DU GITE (FR)	24
EDWARDSTONE	25
EL FABIOLO (FR)	26
ENERGUMENE (FR)	27
ERNE RIVER (IRE)	28
FACILE VEGA (IRE)	28
FERNY HOLLOW (IRE)	30
FIL DOR (FR)	31
FIRST STREET	31
FLOORING PORTER (IRE)	32
GAELIC WARRIOR (GER)	33
GALOPIN DES CHAMPS (FR)	34
GALVIN (IRE)	35
GELINO BELLO (FR)	36
GERICAULT ROQUE (FR)	37
GET IT RIGHT (IRE)	38
GIN COCO (FR)	38
GITCHE GUMEE	39
GOWEL ROAD (IRE)	39
HERMES DU GOUET (FR)	40
HIGHLAND CHARGE (IRE)	41
HILLCREST (IRE)	41

HULLNBACK	42
IL ETAIT TEMPS (FR)	43
JETARA (IRE)	43
JONBON (FR)	44
KATEIRA	45
KILLER KANE (IRE)	46
KNAPPERS HILL (IRE)	46
LAW ELLA (IRE)	47
LEAVE OF ABSENCE (FR)	48
LOOKAWAY (IRE)	48
L'HOMME PRESSE (FR)	49
MAHLER MISSION (IRE)	51
MAJOR DUNDEE (IRE)	51
MARBLE SANDS (FR)	52
MASTER MCSHEE	53
MERLIN GIANT (FR)	54
MIGHTY POTTER (FR)	55
MINELLA COCOONER (IRE)	55
MINELLA CROONER (IRE)	56
MONBEG PARK (IRE)	57
MY DROGO	58
NAME IN LIGHTS (IRE)	58
NORTH LODGE (IRE)	59
NUCKY JOHNSON (IRE)	60
NURSE SUSAN (FR)	60
ODIN'S QUEST	61
OUR POWER (IRE)	62
PARTY BUSINESS (IRE)	62
PATH D'OROUX (FR)	63
PEKING ROSE	64
POETIC MUSIC	64
REDEMPTION DAY	65
SAMARRIVE (FR)	66
SKYTASTIC (FR)	66
SOFT RISK (FR)	67
SOLDIER OF DESTINY (IRE)	68
STATE MAN (FR)	69
STATTLER (IRE)	69
STRINGTOYOURBOW (IRE)	70
SUPER SIX	71
TARAHUMARA	72
TEDDY BLUE (GER)	72
TELMESOMETHINGGIRL (IRE)	73
THE NICE GUY (IRE)	74
UNANSWERED PRAYERS (IRE)	75
WEST CORK WILDWAY (IRE)	76
WESTERN ZARA (IRE)	76
WINTER FOG (IRE)	77

NOTES

NOTES

NOTES

100 WINNERS
HORSES TO FOLLOW FLAT 2023

Companion volume to *100 Winners: Jumpers to Follow*, this book discusses the past performances and future prospects of 100 horses, selected by Raceform's expert race-readers, that are likely to perform well on the Flat in 2023.

To order post the coupon to the address below or order online from **www.racingpost.com/shop**

Tel 01933 304848

ORDER FORM

Please send me a copy of **100 WINNERS: HORSES TO FOLLOW FLAT 2023** as soon as it is published. I enclose a cheque made payable to Pitch Publishing Ltd for **£6.99** (inc p&p)

Name (block capitals) ....

Address ....

....

Postcode ....

SEND TO: PITCH PUBLISHING,

SANDERS ROAD, WELLINGBOROUGH, NORTHANTS NN8 4BX [100F23]